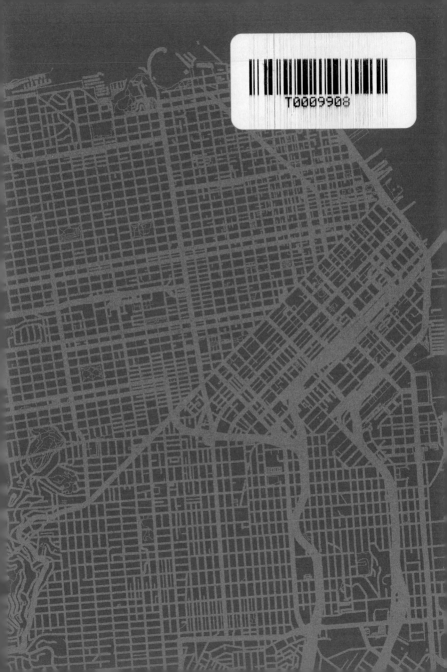

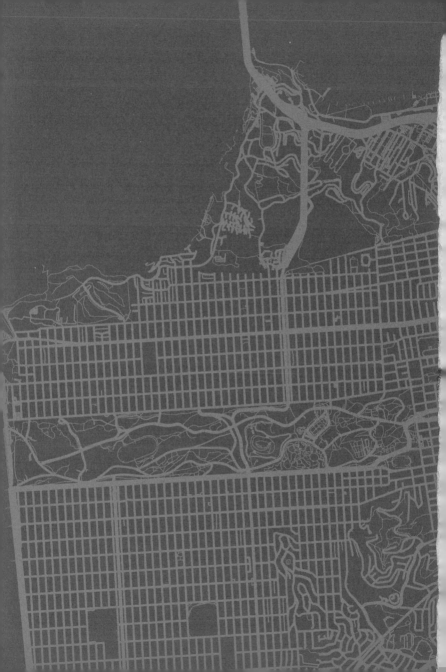

Date Night
SAN FRANCISCO

13-Digit ISBN: 978-1-64643-358-2
10-Digit ISBN: 1-64643-358-0

This book may be ordered by mail from the publisher. Please include $5.99 for postage and handling. Please support your local bookseller first!

Books published by Cider Mill Press Book Publishers are available at special discounts for bulk purchases in the United States by corporations, institutions, and other organizations. For more information, please contact the publisher.

Cider Mill Press Book Publishers
"Where good books are ready for press"
501 Nelson Place
Nashville, Tennessee 37214

cidermillpress.com

Typography: GarageGothic, LiebeLotte, Sofia Pro

All vectors and images used under official license from Shutterstock.com.

Printed in Malaysia

23 24 25 26 27 OFF 5 4 3 2 1
First Edition

Date Night

SAN FRANCISCO

50 Creative, Budget-Friendly Dates for the Golden City

AMY CLEARY

CIDER MILL PRESS

BOOK PUBLISHERS

CONTENTS

♥ INTRODUCTION ♥

Will this book help you find a date? The answer, I am sorry to say, is no. Rather, this book is designed to help you find activities to do on a date. And I'd argue that throwing out a creative idea to the person you have been chatting with on a dating app may be more likely to get a positive response than "let's hang out some-time." In that spirit, I share the best dating advice my father ever gave me: buy two tickets. Why? Because it is often easier to ask someone to go with you to a specific activity than to spend days or weeks trying to come up with a plan. Looking at a calendar for a specific date and time is easier than a vaguer "someday."

The goal of this book is to provide couples, whether they be partners, spouses, or new connections, with ideas for activities that may be a change from the tried and true. Because although it is great to be a regular and have a routine, it is also nice to leave your neighborhood and explore the city, or discover it for the first time with someone with whom you're already in love. The hope is that these dates will help you not only fall in like, or love, or grow your existing relationship with your date, but also to fall in love, or fall in love again, with San Francisco. Working on this project I did as I was visiting new-to-me spots and old favorites.

Of note: although this book is written as a dating guide, there is no reason you cannot do many of these activities with your best friend, a visiting sibling, or your adult child. Just ask my daughter!

San Francisco has lots of pricier activities that you'll find in other guidebooks—usually with five dollar signs attached. You won't find those in this book. Not because they are not great options if you can afford them, but the goal here is to be a bit more accessible. You can have a fun and memorable cheap or free date! However, this is not the be-all and end-all of so-called cheap eats and completely free options. As charm and location were key factors. In general, these dates tend to fall on the more reasonable side of things. That said, there are some relative splurges and I've tried to mention that where they are listed (looking at you, Romantic Restaurants) and to include ways you can make them more afford-able. And remember, costs at bars and restaurants are very dependent upon what you order, especially if you enjoy high-end cocktails or wine.

You'll also see that most of these dates are in San Francisco proper and include most city neighborhoods. Which means that they are designed to be accessible via Muni, foot, bicycle, or rideshare. There are a few options on the Peninsula, in Marin, and in the inner East Bay, but those are mainly also public transportation accessible. I've noted a few where having a car is essential, or at least will be helpful.

This book leans more toward classic than the hottest and the newest. There are three reasons for that. One: with publication lead times, it is not always possible to know what will open and exactly when. Two: places that have been around for a little while are (hopefully) stable and likely to stay open, giving this book a longer life. Three: there are so many great resources for finding out what is hot and new: *Eater*, the *SF Chronicle*, *Thrillist*, *The Infatuation*, and *SFGate* to name a few. Because they can update daily or even hourly, they are always going to be the better option for the coolest, hottest, and newest.

The book is divided into seven themed chapters. Some entries present a fully described date and others take more of a choose-your-own adventure approach, providing multiple options around a theme. The chapters focus on specific attractions or date concepts, which means that there are many popular places across the city not featured, including some of my favorites! So take these ideas as a starting point and explore further.

Clearly, you'll find a lot of different kinds of dates in this book, but what all of them have in common is something that every good date gives you: an opportunity to discover your partner, the city, and yourself in greater depth and intimacy. A shared "Wow" moment when some gorgeous entree is brought to your table; a squeeze of the hand on the ferry to Alcatraz; a sunset view from Bernal Hill that neither of you will ever forget: these little moments add color and joy to the times that we share, making us feel more connected and—dare I say—loved. May all your dates be filled with such moments.

TAKE
A
WALK

Whether it's a trek across the entire city or a stroll through a neighborhood, this chapter presents both highly-planned walks like the Crosstown Trail and The Barbary Coast Trail along with more casual jaunts.

LAND'S END

On the very Western edge of the city, and continent, Land's End is one of the most beautiful spots in the area, offering visitors the sorts of Golden Gate Bridge and ocean views frequently seen on postcards.

The Coastal Trail, a 3-mile-out-and-back hike, is both wildly and deservedly popular. It is also one of the few spots in the Golden Gate National Recreation Area that is dog friendly, so your canine companions can join an outing. What better way to break the ice?

Along the trail, you can enjoy unparalleled coastal views, with spots that cry out for your Instagram grids, not just stories. Keep watch for ruins of old shipwrecks and, in season, migrating whales.

There are spots to stop for a picnic along the way, including three turn-of-the-century gun emplacements at the West Fort Miley batteries.

NOT TO MISS

Look for the slight detour to the Land's End heart, which has replaced the stone labyrinth at a lookout above Mile Rock Beach.

Located at the westernmost point of Land's End, the historic Sutro Baths was once a lavish 25,000-person swimming facility and museum built in the nineteenth century. The facility's six saltwater swimming pools, restaurants, and arcades were enclosed by 100,000 square feet of glass. Destroyed by fire in 1966, Sutro's foundations are visible on the rocks north of the Cliff House (temporarily closed). Trails lead down to the ruins from the nearby parking area.

Daytime dining: Devils Teeth Baking Company on Balboa is famous for its enormous cinnamon roll and breakfast sandwich. Nearby Judah Street has Java Beach, which features exceptional coffee with a quad shot for all of your re-energizing needs. And then there is Outerlands, with one of the best sit-down brunches in town, including a Dutch Pancake (a puffy baked pan-cake) and creative seasonal donuts.

Staying to see the sunset? Red Tavern on Clement is a great spot to warm up with Russian dishes like pelmeni and stroganoff. Craving seafood after the ocean and bay views? Pacific Cafe is a neighborhood classic with complimentary wine while you wait for your seat!

CROSSTOWN TRAIL

Running diagonally across the city, the 17-mile Crosstown Trail is walkable and bikeable. A mix of roads and sidewalks, paved off-road paths, and 40 percent dirt, improved gravel paths and boardwalks, it has about 2,600 feet of elevation gain heading in either direction. For reference, the popular hiking app AllTrails classifies it

♥ Sutro Baths

as moderate, though some sections are more challenging than others.

You can do the whole trail for a full-day experience, but for a more manageable walk, the trail can be divided into five segments.

Heading north, the five sections are:

Section 1: Candlestick Point, Visitacion Valley, McLaren Park:

The first section of the trail, which is 5.2 miles, takes you through neighborhoods many are less familiar with. Beginning at Sunrise Point Fishing Pier in the Candlestick Point State Recreation Area, the route includes the Visitacion Valley Greenway, which is a perfect spot for a break at one of the benches or tile tables, and McLaren Park before passing near Alemany Farm on the way to Glen Park.

OF NOTE

If you are doing the hike Monday-Saturday, visit Mission Blue near the Visitacion Valley Greenway for trail enthusiasm plus coffee and tea, hot or iced, and pastries. Farther along, the main stretch of Glen Park along Diamond Street is a great place to dine. Depending upon time of day and if you are continuing on, top spots include Gialina for pizza (dinner only) or Canyon Market for sandwiches, trail snacks, and more.

Section 2: Glen Park Greenway, Glen Canyon Park, Laguna Honda Trail

This three-mile hike is considered the easiest on the trail. It takes you along some of the nicest pathways, including Glen Canyon Park, an almost 70-acre tree-filled greenway that is a dog walker's and urban hiker's paradise. The views of Sutro Tower are a highlight of this route, but also the delightful forested trails behind Laguna Honda Hospital. There are fewer places to stop for treats along this route, so picking up supplies from Canyon Market at the start and enjoying a picnic in the Canyon is a good plan.

Section 3: Golden Gate Heights Park, Grandview Park, Tiled Stairways (2.1 miles)

This 2.1-mile portion of the train has been called the stair section. You'll reach the top of the 16th Avenue Tiled Steps, with 360-degree views and one of the best-known spots on the trail. While this segment is shorter than most, it's rigorous, with many flights of stairs. Cyclists who don't want to carry their bikes up and down should use an alternate route. This route ends at 16th and Judah, which leaves you just around the corner from Sam Tung and some of the best chicken wings in San Francisco. If you are continuing on and want something handheld, Pineapple King Bakery is a great spot to grab a classic bun or tart.

♥ Japanese Tea Garden

Section 4 runs for 2.2 miles along the eastern side of Golden Gate Park, including Stow Lake, the rose garden, and the Japanese Tea Garden before reaching the Park Presidio Greenway. As you cross Geary and Clement, you will find many options for sit-down restaurants or items to carry along the trail for a picnic. In particular, Breadbelly is a short detour on Clement.

The trail continues for 3.8 miles into the Presidio, a 1,500-acre collection of natural and cultural treasures. On this leg of the journey, you'll pass the Legion of Honor museum, as well as the USS San Francisco Memorial. You'll end your day (or start it if you are heading southbound) at Land's End (see page 14).

PHILOSOPHER'S WAY

Can you call a 318-acre park that is San Francisco's second largest a secret? Maybe, if it is in a neighborhood on the southeast side of the city, far from tourist hubs and off the radar even for many locals. Established in 1927, the park is named for John McLaren, the "grandfather" of Golden Gate Park. In addition to playgrounds, picnic areas, and game courts, you'll find the Jerry

Garcia Amphitheater, a golf course, and McNab Lake. You can explore scenic meadows, grasslands, and wetland habitat with more than 7 miles of walking trails.

The Philosopher's Way is a 2.7-mile trail around the perimeter of the park. Dedicated in 2013, it is the first and only path built for philosophers in the United States, inspired by similar walks found in cities such as Heidelberg, Toronto, and Kyoto. According to the trail designers, "these are places where poets, philosophers, and intellectuals strolled through in conversation, considering the ideas of their times."

NOT TO MISS

Built in 1956, the eighty-foot-tall, 350,000-gallon blue water tower is hard to miss. With a panoramic vista spanning San Bruno to downtown San Francisco, including great views of Twin Peaks and Mount Davidson, it is a perfect picnic spot.

The Jerry Garcia Amphitheater is a Greek-style venue that hosts a variety of outdoor concerts and events throughout the year. It's named in honor of Jerry Garcia of the The Grateful Dead, who grew up nearby in the Excelsior.

You follow the stone arrows to 14 "musing" stations, featuring plaques with a quotation, a bit of park history, or other trivia. The project was a partnership between the San Francisco Arts Commission and the San Francisco Public Utilities Commission. The trailhead is located at 1229 Mansell Street.

- Roxie Food Center has been a San Francisco sandwich favorite for almost 50 years. You can personalize as much as you would like (Dutch Crunch highly recommended!), or try one of their combos, including the turkey and pastrami Simon special or Roxie special with ham, mortadella, salami, American, and Swiss cheese and artichokes.

- If your sandwich of choice is more of a banh mi, TY Sandwiches is a great pre- or post-park spot.

- Have you ever wanted to make a meal of just deli salads? If so, The Salad Place is the spot for you. Mix and match a combo of four for a fun meal or go for a sandwich.

- If you are looking for a classic Italian deli sandwich, like the Mark with prosciutto, imported mortadella, pepper salame, hot coppa, fresh mozzarella, roasted peppers, pepperoncini, oil and vinegar, Calabria Bros. is the spot for you.

- Skipping the picnic? Gentilly has a menu of Cajun flavors and excellent cocktails, with a weekday happy hour, weekend brunch, and dinner. Broken Record is a dive bar with cocktails and a history of excellent food, and is a great spot to warm up after your walk.

BARBARY COAST TRAIL

If you're a local, it is likely that you have seen one of the brass medallions with arrows on your commute, or on your way to meet friends downtown. Inspired by the Freedom Trail in Boston, the Barbary Coast Trail is a 3.8-mile historical walking trail designated by 180 bronze medallions and arrows embedded in the sidewalk connecting 20 historical sites. The trail focuses on the period between the Gold Rush and the 1906 earthquake and fire, but also highlights more recent history, like the 1950s in North Beach.

The trail begins at the Old Mint at 5th and Mission Streets before heading through Union Square, Chinatown, Montgomery Street, Jackson Square, North Beach, Telegraph Hill, Fisherman's Wharf, and Aquatic Park. The northern end of the trail is at the San Francisco Maritime National Historical Park.

Sites along the trail include: the Old Mint, Union Square, Old St. Mary's (the first Catholic cathedral west of the Rockies), T'ien Hou Temple (the first Asian temple in North America), Jackson Square Historic District (which contains the last cluster of Gold Rush and Barbary Coast–era buildings in town), Old Ship Saloon (once a shanghaiing den), City Lights Bookstore, Coit Tower, and the Buena Vista Cafe.

♥ Coit Tower

- **Wayfare Tavern:** Slightly off the trail but very much in the spirit, Wayfare is a take on a classic American tavern, with some of the best deviled eggs, pop-overs, and fried chicken around. You can sit at the bar, people watch, and share.

- **Eastern Bakery:** Chinatown's oldest bakery, Eastern features coffee crunch cake as well as pork buns, mooncakes, and more.

- **Golden Gate Fortune Cookie Factory:** It's hard to resist the scent of baking cookies at this sweet spot, which has been in business since 1962 and still makes fortune cookies the old-fashioned way, by hand. Plus, you can make your own fortune, creating a great romantic memento.

- **Bix:** If you are doing this walk in the evening, this is a charming spot to stop for a classic cocktail.

- **Cotogna:** Also in the Jackson Square neighborhood, Cotogna is a favorite of many and has one of the prettiest parklets in town. To keep things on budget, share a pasta and pizza.

- **Comstock Saloon:** Founded in 1907, this bar sits at the crossroads of North Beach, Chinatown, and Jackson Square, and is the perfect spot to enjoy some history with your drink and snacks.

- **Maison Nico:** Located steps from the Transamerica Pyramid, this modern épicerie and café serves pâté en croûte, brioche feuilletée, and more.

For North Beach suggestions see page 57.

STAIRCASES

Entire books have been written about the famous and lesser-known staircases of San Francisco, and if you enjoy exploring the city's neighborhoods, they are well worth a read. See page 194 for some great places to pick up such a book (and loads more).

The good thing about a staircase: the views. The bad thing: they can be challenging, so don't forget to stop and enjoy the views as you climb. Here are a few of the city's highlights.

- **Greenwich Steps:** The lesser known of the two sets of steps leading to Coit Tower. See more on page 56. Start near the corner of Greenwich and Sansome.

- **Filbert Steps:** One of the most famous sets of steps in the city, the Filbert Steps rise in three sections from Sansome Street to Coit Tower.

- **Lincoln Park Steps:** Local artist Aileen Barr created mesmerizing art steps with bright colors, tropical themes, and a captivating design. At the top of the stairs, you can see Salesforce Tower and the Golden Gate Bridge.

- **16th Avenue Tiled Steps:** Sometimes called the Hidden Garden Steps, this staircase runs from

♥ Lincoln Park Steps

Kirkham to Lawton Streets, with beautiful tile artwork on the front of them.

- **Lyon Street Steps:** The Lyon Street Steps connect Cow Hollow to Pacific Heights as well as the Presidio's Broadway Gate. They are very popular with trainers and solo exercisers.

- **Vulcan Stairs:** This two-block stretch of concrete stairs connects Levant and Ord Streets, and is lined with carefully tended gardens and gorgeous homes. The nearby, shorter Saturn Street Steps connect Saturn and Ord Streets. A little park sits at the base on Ord Street, giving you a great place to rest.

- **Arelious Walker Stairway:** Located in the Bayview, this staircase pays homage to Dr. Arelious Walker, a pastor and neighborhood advocate. The 87 steps are decorated with textiles and ceramics from Africa, Central America, and the Middle East.

- **Fillmore Street Steps:** Connecting Pacific Heights to Cow Hollow and the Marina, these steps were originally built in 1915 for the Panama-Pacific International Exhibition and are carved into the sidewalk. At the summit at the intersection of Fillmore Street and Broadway, you can get a view of the Golden Gate Bridge, Alcatraz, and the Palace of Fine Arts.

- **Tompkins Stairway Garden:** Just up the hill from the Alemany Farmers Market, this park features a drought-tolerant garden in year-round bloom and a colorful tiled stairway.

TREE WALK

Cherry trees are considered a sign of good fortune when in bloom and also stand for love and romance. Redwood trees represent eternity, whereas maple trees symbolize balance, strength, and endurance—all things we are looking for in a good relationship! So, why not a romantic neighborhood tree walk?

The city's Landmark tree program is a great way to start. "Landmark" trees, it turns out, are designated by the Board of Supervisors for their environmental, cultural, historical, botanical, or other importance. The landmarking process requires extensive assessment by the Urban Forestry Council, based on a set of specific criteria. These trees can be on public or private land and the city's website has a handy map.

If you are looking for something more structured, the knowledgeable and creative team behind San Francisco Trees has some ideas for you. Michael Sullivan, one of the trio behind the site, wrote a book on San Francisco trees, and during the pandemic, along with Richard Turner and Jason Dewees, he created sidewalk-chalked

♥ Golden Gate Park

tours in neighborhoods across the city. Because sidewalk chalk tends to wear off, they memorialized the tours with directions and tree details on their website: sftrees. com. There you can find dozens of tours, as well as their list of San Francisco's top trees, if you'd prefer more of a scavenger hunt approach. It is a great way to learn more about a neighborhood.

For something even simpler, why not explore the trees depending on the season? Spend the spring finding the magnolias or search for signs of fall color in autumn.

BAYVIEW/ HUNTERS POINT

For some, Bayview/Hunters Point remains an undiscovered part of San Francisco. Often called the city's sunniest neighborhood, it is home to waterfront parks, a creative scene, and a significant legacy of African American religious, civic, cultural, athletic, and educational achievements.

- **Heron's Head Park:** Named for its resemblance to the Great Blue Heron when viewed from the air, this 22-acre open space is home to a thriving wildlife habitat, attracting more than 100 bird species a year.

- **Hunters Point Shoreline Park:** Walk through here for a fascinating look at the history of the area to get to India Basin Shoreline Park. Only 150 years ago, the San Francisco Bay was ringed by wetlands that supported many plant and animal species. Over 90 percent of these wetlands have been lost to development, but India Basin remains as the only natural area within the San Francisco Recreation and Parks Department system that borders the bay. Work on this project is ongoing, but you can already see what an asset it will be to the neighborhood and city as a whole.

- **Arelious Walker Stairway:** These mosaic steps, known as "Flights of Fancy," pay homage to Dr. Arelious Walker, a pastor and neighborhood advocate. The stairs use textiles and ceramics from Africa, Central America, and the Middle East.

- **Bayview Opera House:** The Opera House is San Francisco's oldest theater and a registered historical landmark. More than just a building, it is operated as a community cultural and arts center by the nonprofit Bayview Opera House Inc. and holds a significant place in the neighborhood's history and culture.

- **Flora Grubb Garden:** This garden, design, house-plant, furniture, and home decor store is simply a fun place to explore.

- **Archimedes Banya:** Archimedes Banya is a blend of the traditions of Greek laconica, Turkish hammam, German thermen, and Russian banya combined with science and technology to create an experience like no other. They offer detoxing, plunges into an ice-cold pool, and more.

- **Bay Natives:** This nursery has offered California native plants for the urban landscape since 2005. Don't miss City Grazing's goats next door for a chance to see the hillside-cleaning creatures up close.

- **Old Skool Cafe:** This jazzy 1920s-styled supper club is run by youth coming out of the system of incarceration, foster care, and other challenging situations. The cuisine is international soul food—comfort food from around the world, celebrating favorite family recipes from the youth involved. Dinner is accompanied by live entertainment, from jazz to classical and everything in between.

- **Tato:** Named after the owner's son, this tacos-and-more spot pays homage to the family roots in Mexico City. They use locally sourced ingredients to make the recipes of Tato's abuelita, combined with delicious ideas discovered during their travels.

- **All Good Pizza:** From the same owners as Tato, All Good is built around a brick pizza oven housed in a shipping container. The Neapolitan-style pizzas topped with local vegetables and meats are served on picnic tables in their beer garden.

- **Auntie April's Chicken, Waffles, & Soul Food Restaurant:** Serving fried chicken and waffles, as well as braised oxtails, red beans and rice, and shrimp po'boys.

- **Frisco Fried:** Home of some of the best fried chicken in San Francisco, Frisco Fried also features fried fish, oysters, and prawns.

- **Speakeasy:** The Prohibition era-themed taproom features their core line of beers brewed in-house, along with seasonal offerings and one-offs from their Brewery, not to mention guest taps from other breweries.

- **Radio African Kitchen:** Come here for a blend of North African, Mediterranean, and Ethiopian flavors on a regularly changing menu.

- **Laughing Monk:** This small-batch brewery features inventive California-meets-Belgian-style beer, but also frequent activities like trivia, pinball, collaborations with other breweries, and food trucks. In their words, they "are traditionally irreverent, inspired by the pastimes of Belgium, but always in the spirit of California's innovative mindset."

IN THE PARKS

San Francisco has more than 200 parks. In fact, the Trust for Public Land has found that 100 percent of San Franciscans live within a 10-minute walk of a park and that 21 percent of San Francisco's city land is used for parks and recreation. This section offers ideas on how to enjoy these local treasures, as well as the Presidio and the Golden Gate National Recreation Area.

GARDEN OF SHAKESPEARE'S FLOWERS

It may seem strange to call one of the most popular weddings sites in Golden Gate Park a hidden gem, but this secluded garden often feels that way. Located near the 9th Avenue entrance to the park, the garden was the brainchild of the California Spring Blossom and Wildflower Association, which proposed plans for a garden filled with flowers mentioned in the works of William Shakespeare. Nearly 100 years later it continues to delight visitors.

More intimate than the neighboring Botanical Gardens, it is harder to think of a more lovely spot for a picnic, with or without reading aloud your favorite play or sonnet. The charming iron gate entrance opens into a walled garden of more than 200 flowers and plants, a sundial, bronze plaques featuring notable quotations, and a bust of the Bard himself overlooking it all. There are benches to sit on and plenty of lawn space to spread out.

For Your Picnic

The closest dining stretch to the Shakespeare Garden is 9th Avenue, which has options from sushi to burritos to burgers. It would be hard to look past Tartine Inner

Sunset, where treats may include smoked salmon or turkey sandwiches, quiche, Almond Lemon Tea Cake, and seasonal fresh-fruit tarts.

Planning ahead? With 24-hours notice, enjoy a full to-go afternoon tea from Sip Tea Room, although smaller options are available for grab and go on the weekends.

ADD ON

Take a short walk through the Music Concourse, where there are frequent live performances. No show? Keep walking to The Hamon Observation Tower at the de Young Museum. Open Tuesday through Sunday from 9:30am to 4:30pm, it offers a spectacular glass-walled space with 360-degree panoramic views of downtown San Francisco, Golden Gate Park, the Bay, and the Marin Headlands. Tickets are not required.

Steps from the tower is the SkyStar Wheel. Standing 150 feet tall, SkyStar Wheel boasts, on non-foggy days, views spanning from downtown San Francisco to the Pacific Ocean. Installed in 2020 as part of Golden Gate Park's 150th anniversary celebration, it will remain in San Francisco until March 2025. Tickets are required and advance purchase is recommended.

♥ Garden of Shakespeare's Flowers

DOLORES PARK

Many San Franciscans think the best way to spend a sunny day is on a picnic blanket or towel in Dolores Park, people watching and hanging out. The park features green lawn, tennis courts, a basketball court, a playground, and two off-leash dog play areas and hosts many festivals, performances, and other cultural events.

Dolores Park has become a hangout for the whole city and attracts as many locals as out-of-town visitors. So if you are heading there on a beautiful day, expect a crowd. Parking can be difficult, so if possible, take Muni's J line or other public transportation. Bathroom lines can be long, so be patient. Trash left in the park after a busy weekend has become a problem, so you are encouraged to pack out trash and recyclables. There are no food facilities in the park itself, but there are often food vendors, both of the family-friendly and 420-friendly sorts.

♥ For Your Picnic

Bi-Rite Market, one of the city's favorite gourmet groceries, is right down 18th Street, with some of the best sandwiches, deli items, wine, and cheese in town. Just slightly farther down the street you will find both Pizzeria Delfina for a takeout pizza that will be the envy of your park neighbors, as well as Tartine for sandwiches and pastries. If you are there on a weekday, don't miss the creative sandwiches at Turner's Kitchen, located at 3505 17th St. Similarly, Rhea's Deli on Valencia Street offers a memorable Korean steak sandwich as well as numerous offerings named after local streets and neighborhoods.

Don't forget that if you are coming from BART, or willing to walk a few blocks, you'll have access to an overwhelming array of excellent burritos.

Making a day and night of it? The 500 Club has long been one of the best dive bars in San Francisco and is located very near the park at 500 Guerrero St. A bit farther away on 16th St. is ABV, recently named one of North America's 50 Best Bars by the team behind the publication *World's 50 Best Bars*. Plus, their food and cocktails are worth the walk.

STOP AND SMELL THE ROSES

Roses may be a Valentine's Day cliché, but in the Bay Area, you can picnic or walk in a rose garden. Even those who think of themselves as too cool for roses will revel in the scents and often delightful names of the flowers in these fragrant gardens. Pick your favorites and marvel at the variety of colors and types.

- **Rose Garden:** In San Francisco, the Rose Garden is located in Golden Gate Park at John F. Kennedy Drive and 14th Avenue. The garden features more than 60 rose beds and full bloom is generally May through June. That said, some roses bloom twice a year, so even in non-peak times you may catch some blooms.

- **Berkeley Rose Garden:** Located next to Codornices Park, the Berkeley Rose Garden was a WPA project that originally opened to the public in 1937. Its three acres of rose beds are planted along wonderful views of the Bay and Golden Gate Bridge on clear days. Peak bloom is generally mid-May. While there, don't miss the long concrete slide at Codornices Park.

- **Morcom Rose Garden:** Oakland's rose garden is an eight-acre garden with more than 6,000 rose bushes. Bloom can last from late April through October. Located in a residential neighborhood

PRO TIP

JFK Drive in Golden Gate Park is permanently closed to car traffic. If you are looking to explore other areas of the park while there, you can ride the free shuttle that operates seven days a week from Haight and Stanyan Streets, along JFK Drive, to Transverse Drive, with stops along the way at some of the park's most popular attractions.

near Piedmont, it also features a reflecting pool and fountains. Nearby Grand and Oakland Avenues have many food and drink options.

- **Filoli:** Located a little farther out of town in Woodside on the Peninsula, Filoli features 654 acres that were originally a private residence. The property is considered one of the finest remaining country estates of the twentieth century, with a Georgian revival-style mansion, 16 acres of English Renaissance gardens, a 6.8-acre Gentleman's Orchard, and hundreds of acres of natural lands. It was also the TV home of the Carrington family on the 1980s show *Dynasty*! Roses can be in bloom April through October, but visits at other times can include a spectacular tulip display, camellias, magnolias, and elaborate holiday decorations.

TAKE IN A (NATURAL) LIGHT SHOW

Sunrise, sunset. Sunrise, sunset. Whichever you prefer, San Francisco has many spots for you.

A dawn date? For the early birds or those still up from the night before, sunrise is a great chance to enjoy a generally uncrowded view, with or without coffee, mimosas, and croissants. It can lead to a day together spent exploring the city or simply a stunning photo.

Two of the best sunrises in the city can be found at Bernal Heights Park and Corona Heights Park.

Bernal Heights Park: With a 360-degree panorama and clear views of San Francisco Bay, the Golden Gate Bridge, downtown, San Bruno Mountain, and the hills of the East Bay, Bernal Heights Park features a paved access road to get you to trails that lead to the summit. Once the sun is up, don't miss neighborhood gem Black Jet Baking Company for seasonal fruit danishes and Pat Greaney breakfast sandwiches.

Corona Heights Park: Located above the Castro, a one-mile trail network winds around the hill and takes you up to the summit with a 360-degree view of the Bay Area. To complete a romantic morning, head to Cole Valley's

Zazie for gingerbread pancakes or one of eight Benedict options.

More of a night owl than a morning person? Looking to recreate the sunset kiss from many films? Luckily, San Francisco has a long list of optimal sunsets spots. Here are some favorites:

- **Crissy Field and the Tunnel Tops:** Looking for a sunset with the Golden Gate Bridge, many picnic spots, and a flat walking path? Look no further than Crissy Field. This is the perfect spot to bring a blanket, wine, and cheese and marvel. If you'd like this view with a bit more elevation and an available fire pit, climb to the new Tunnel Tops Park.

- **Ocean Beach:** Watch the sun set over the Pacific with great reflections of the colors on the incoming waves. Be warned, it is often chilly at the beach, so bring blankets for cuddling. For more on Ocean Beach see page 140.

- **Land's End:** Another Golden Gate Bridge sunset, this one with a little bit of elevation. For more on Land's End see page 14.

- **Baker Beach** is the most popular beach in the Presidio and offers stunning views of the Marin Headlands and Golden Gate Bridge. A great picnic option is a stop at Pizzetta 211 for a pizza and cheeseboard to share.

- **Twin Peaks:** In the center of the city and towering over it all, the views span from Ocean Beach and the Golden Gate Bridge to the Mission District and Potrero Hill and beyond. For a warming meal after the sun goes down, head to Anchor Oyster Bar for a memorable version of San Francisco's classic fish soup, cioppino.

- **Alamo Square Park:** Turn east to see the city skyline behind the famous Painted Ladies. Turn west to see the sunset. Note: this is also a great sunrise option. Afterward, walk down the hill to Divisadero Street for a large selection of food and drink options.

- **Alta Plaza Park:** Climb the broad, tiered staircase up the terraced southern slope of this steep hillside park to find panoramic views of the city and bay that delight both at sunrise and sunset. Walk down to nearby Fillmore Street for a post-sunset drink.

- **Francisco Park:** One of the city's newest parks, this was built on the site of a long-abandoned reservoir at the bottom of Russian Hill. The 4.5-acre site includes a large lawn, a community garden, a dog park, and extraordinary bay views, stretching from the Golden Gate to Aquatic Park and Alcatraz. Ghirardelli Square is a short walk if you'd like to finish your evening with a hot fudge sundae.

THE PRESIDIO

A 1,500-acre former military base, the Presidio has become San Francisco's playground and one of America's most popular national park sites. The park features incredible views, outdoor art installations, hikes, museums, and much more, including a classic 12-lane bowling alley.

Top things to do in the park include:

- Exploring Andy Goldsworthy's outdoor art installations The Spire, Wood Libe, Tree Fall, and Earth Wall, which can be visited individually or enjoyed together via a three-mile hiking loop along the Presidio's trail network.

- Hanging out on some of the city's top beaches, including Baker Beach with its amazing Golden Gate Bridge views, the lesser-known, secluded Marshall Beach, and Crissy Field East Beach, one of the best picnic spots in the park.

- Hiking the miles of trails for both a leisurely stroll or a true workout. Of note for romantics: the oldest footpath through the Presidio, Lovers Lane, connects the Presidio Gate to the Main Post.

- Visiting the Walt Disney Museum for its meticulously planned journey through Disney's fascinating life. The permanent galleries offer deep insight into his creative risks, failures, and triumphs thanks to personal artifacts belonging to the pioneering animator and his family, including the first-known drawing of a certain mouse.

- Learn about the history of San Francisco and the Presidio at spots like the Battery East, World War II Memorial, and San Francisco National Cemetery. Plus you can visit two of the remaining earthquake shacks from 1906.

- Impressing your date with your knowledge of the area by showing them Presidio Pet Cemetery, one of the quirkiest spots in the park. Located where McDowell Avenue meets Crissy Field Avenue beneath the new Presidio Parkway viaduct, this is a reminder of the military families that lived at the

Presidio Hiking Trail

Presidio when it was an army base.

- Admiring Fort Point, a must-see for fans of history, architecture, and those looking for a very close up view of the Golden Gate Bridge—from underneath. Movie fans may recognize it from Hitchock's *Vertigo*.

- Bowling at Presidio Bowl, replete with 12 lanes, over 45 beers, 19 wines by the glass, and a very popular burger. Friday and Saturday nights feature glow-in-the-dark bowling!

Eat & Drink:

- **Colibri Mexican Bistro:** Located in the historic Officers' Club, Colibri serves up authentic Mexican cuisine, including mole, pozole, and carnitas, as well as a set of rotating specials that can be enjoyed during lunch, dinner, weekend brunch, and happy hour either inside or on the spacious patio.

- **Presidio Social Club:** A modern take on old-school American dining.

- **The Warming Hut:** Pick up souvenirs as well as snacks and a delightful hot chocolate for when the fog rolls in.

- **Sessions:** Located in the Letterman Digital Arts Center, Sessions has a patio with postcard views of the Golden Gate Bridge and is known for its large selection of beers.

- **Tunnel Tops and Battery Bluff Parks:** Opened in 2022, Battery Bluff and Tunnel Tops parks are the two newest spots to explore with Golden Gate Bridge views from scenic overlooks, firepits, and charming paths through gardens and meadows, plus a playground that will make you wish you were a child again. As of this writing, restaurants are planned for the site, but for now the Presidio is featuring an ongoing variety of mobile food providers, including trucks, carts, and tents operating on a rotating schedule seven days a week from 9:00am to 6:00pm. As a bonus, there are also strategically placed tables and benches, in case you forgot your picnic blanket.

Battery Bluff Park is a six-acre spot along the Presidio Promenade trail near San Francisco National Cemetery that blends history, nature, and incredible views of the Golden Gate Bridge. It is a great picnic spot that also features benches placed to highlight the views.

PRO TIP

On Friday nights, don't miss Off the Grid at the Fort Mason Center, the first food truck market in California, featuring a full bar and live music throughout the season. Plus, it is one of the largest food truck gatherings of its kind in the United States, so there is something for everyone.

SALESFORCE PARK

Although it sounds like a sports stadium, Salesforce Park is actually an urban park located on top of downtown's transit center. About four blocks long, the 5-acre rooftop park, accessible by escalator or gondole, features 600 trees and 16,000 plants in 13 small botanical gardens with flora and fauna representing different regions of the world, and a bus fountain designed to correspond with the arrivals and departures of the buses below. The park hosts a collection of free events every week, including yoga classes, bootcamps, live music, bird walks, and garden tours.

Why is Salesforce Park a great place for a date? It feels very much like a hidden escape in one of the more urban parts of the city, making it a convenient spot for a workday lunch or post-work meet up. You can bring a picnic and feel like you have gotten away from it all only steps from downtown offices. Conveniently located in the transit center are Venga Empanadas and AndyTown Coffee for drinks and delightful pastries. More restaurants are scheduled to open soon.

Looking for other hidden spots downtown? Even locals may have not heard of POPOS. What are they? POPOS (privately owned public open spaces) are publicly accessible spaces in the form of plazas, terraces, atriums, and small parks, which are provided and

♥ Salesforce Park

maintained by private developers. In San Francisco, POPOS mostly appear in the downtown office district area. They include Transamerica Redwood Park, the rooftop sun terraces on the Crocker Galleria, and a 5-story greenhouse at 101 Second St. You can see a full list at sfpopos.com.

For more flowers downtown, check out Union Square in Bloom, which runs March through June. Union Square will be full of bright, beautiful flowers with floral displays throughout the district. Winter Wanderland in Union Square is inspired by European holiday

PRO TIP

Note that the tower is only open until early evening, so make this your first stop on an evening date.

markets, featuring local handmade gifts, holiday tree decorations, sweets, and warming drinks, as well as live entertainment, Santa's Workshop, and a seasonal ice rink.

CITY LIGHTS BOOKSTORE

Founded by poet Lawrence Ferlinghetti and Peter D. Martin, City Lights remains a truly great independent bookstore, a place where booklovers from across the country and around the world come to browse, read, and just soak in the ambiance of alternative culture's only "Literary Landmark." The store calls itself "a literary meeting place since 1953" and offers three floors of both new releases from all of the major publishing houses, along with an impressive range of titles from smaller, harder-to-find, specialty publishers. City Lights is also a publisher whose press produces a dozen or so titles a year, and they host regular author events.

Step outside to see the Zapatista Mural in Kerouac Alley that recreates a piece of community artwork that was destroyed in April 1998 when armed forces violently attacked the indigenous village of Taniperla, a Zapatista community in Chiapas, Mexico.

COIT TOWER

The San Francisco skyline has changed significantly in recent years. But much like Sutro Tower and the Transamerica Pyramid, the 210-foot Coit Tower remains an unmistakable emblem of San Francisco's skyline.

Completed in 1933, its observation deck provides 360-degree views of the city and bay. The tower is named for Lillie Hitchcock Coit, a wealthy eccentric and patron of the city's firefighters. Coit died in 1929, leaving a substantial bequest "for the purpose of adding to the beauty of the city I have always loved." The murals inside the tower's base were painted in 1934 by a group of artists employed by the Public Works of Art Project, a precursor to the Works Progress Administration (WPA), and depict life in California during the Depression. You can visit the murals for free or buy a $4 ticket to take an elevator to the observation deck. For a scenic hike to the tower, climb Telegraph Hill's eastern slope via the Filbert Street Steps or the Greenwich Street Steps.

Eat & Drink

Often mentioned in travel guides as San Francisco's Little Italy, North Beach has a high density of both classic restaurants, cafes, and bars and more timely recent additions.

- **Caffe Trieste:** The first espresso coffee house established on the West Coast in 1956 is famous as a hub for writers and has been called the heartbeat of North Beach.

- **Vesuvio Cafe:** Just across Jack Kerouac Alley from City Lights, this living monument to jazz, poetry, and art was established in 1948, and was a hangout for the likes of Kerouac, Allen Ginsberg, Lawrence

Coit Tower

Ferlinghetti, and Neal Cassady. Grab a drink and take a seat at a table by the second-floor windows for some of the best people watching around.

- **Original Joe's:** This family-owned spot is a favorite of tourists and locals alike for large plates of classic Italian American comfort food.

- **Tony's Pizza Napoletana:** Learn a lot about your date as you see which pizza they select from this menu of a dozen American and Italian pizza styles.

- **Liguria Bakery:** Open for limited hours, this is the place to find the focaccia of your dreams for a picnic in Washington Square Park.

- **Mario's Bohemian Cigar Store Cafe:** There is a full menu but you're really here for a meatball or eggplant sandwich. Get both and share!

- **Red Window:** Looking for something beyond Italian? This Spanish low-proof cocktail and tapas spot feels like a party.

- **Sotto Mare:** Start with oysters and share Cioppino at the classic seafood spot.

- **Golden Boy Pizza:** A large and inexpensive slice of Sicilian pizza that is a great stop pre- or post-cocktails.

- **Molinari Delicatessen:** This old-school deli is a prime spot to load up for a Washington Square Park picnic.

- **Freddie's Sandwiches:** Another top contender for a park sandwich, Freddie's features over 30 varieties of sandwiches packed with high-quality meats and cheeses. Breakfast and lunch only.

- **Cassava:** New to North Beach, Cassava was previously an Outer Richmond favorite for brunch and dinner. Their Japanese breakfast, with rice, vegetables, pickles, salmon, miso soup, house furikake, and a soft poached egg is a highlight.

BOTANICAL GARDEN

San Francisco Botanical Garden is a treasure. Not only does it offer 55 acres of beautiful gardens, displaying nearly 9,000 kinds of plants from around the world, but it is free for San Francisco residents. You can picnic on many of the wide lawns, lose yourself wandering the many trails, or take a docent-led tour. Because of our climate, the garden is a delight year-round, but also hosts numerous special events throughout the year from yoga to plant sales to musical performances. And although it is called San Francisco Botanical Garden, it is really a collection of multiple gardens (as of 2022, the Botanical Garden has joined with the Japanese Tea

♥ **Conservatory of Flowers**

Garden and Conservatory of Flowers under the Gardens of Golden Gate Park umbrella; all three are now free for SF residents and out-of-towners can buy a single pass).

Explore regions from Chile to Australia to the Mediterranean to Temperate Asia or focus on themed gardens like the Garden of Fragrance, Succulent Garden, or Ancient Plants.

- **Magnificent Magnolias:** When you call them Magnificent Magnolias, you set expectations pretty high, but this annual display exceeds them. The most significant conservation collection of magnolias in the United States, the trees bloom January through March. The garden features more than

200 magnolia trees, in pink, white, and magenta. Because the trees bloom at different times, you can go back week after week for a new display. Of particular note is a tree known as "Darjeeling." Thought by many to be the most spectacular of all the magnolias at the Garden, this Himalayan selection was propagated from a tree at Lloyd Botanic Garden in Darjeeling, India, and puts on a dramatic display of magnificent deep-pink flowers emerging on leafless branches.

- **Flower Piano:** Likely the most popular annual event at the Garden, Flower Piano features multiple pianos placed around the garden grounds. The event typically takes place in September and there are scheduled performances, but also the opportunity for amateurs to take a turn when the pianos are free. You can spend a full day at one garden, or wander on a piano scavenger hunt from one garden to the next. Impromptu serenade, anyone?

- **Dahlia Garden:** Not in the Botanical Garden, but instead located near the Conservatory of Flowers, Dahlia Garden celebrates the official flower of San Francisco with a diverse spread of colors that grow in a thick, fenced-in treasure trove of blooms. They start to bloom in June and reach their peak level of beauty in late August and September.

There are many great takeout options nearby, including several dim sum options listed on page 82, but a stop at Arguello Super Market for a turkey sandwich on Dutch crunch plus chips or deli salad of your choice is an excellent and convenient option. Look for the sign that says: "World's best turkey sandwich."

Another option on your way in or out of the park is Lily on Clement for banh mi and more. Their weekend set brunch with an appetizer, entrée, and drink is a great way to go. Don't miss the refreshing Preserved Lime Sinh To with salty lime, kumquat, yogurt, and pomegranate.

FOR THE FOODIE

Rankings may change slightly from year to year, but San Francisco is one of the most restaurant-dense cities in the country. In particular, San Francisco is independent-restaurant dense, and most local favorites are independently owned or part of small local restaurant groups. Which means that there are a lot of options to explore!

TACO CRAWL

San Francisco loves tacos. From food trucks to sidewalk stands and sit-down restaurants, the city is full of great spots. It is also a city where many people have very strong opinions on tacos, making a taco crawl a great way to share favorites with a date and give yourselves something to taco about.

There is no way to list even a sliver of all the city's excellent taco options, but here are a few suggestions to use as a jumping off point:

- **La Taqueria:** Named an American Classic by the James Beard Awards, La Taqueria has been a Mission Street highlight for almost 50 years. Pro tip: ask for your taco (or burrito) to be prepared dorado style and it will be crisped on the grill.

- **La Palma:** Open since 1953, La Palma is often seen as a place for house-made tortillas, plus Latin groceries, but the tacos made on those tortillas are very much worth a walk down 24th Street. Plus, you can take home salsas, guacamole, and prepared foods for later.

- **Belman La Gallinita Meat Market:** Established in 1965, this meat market, with prepared foods, remains family owned. The cecina is highly recommended.

- **Gallo Giro:** Located at 23rd Street and Treat Avenue on weekdays, this truck is particularly known for its carnitas.

- **Taqueria Vallarta:** This is the spot for less common tacos, like buche (pork stomach) or suadero (a cut of beef), but you also won't go wrong with carne asada or pollo asado. Don't miss the salsa bar.

- **Tacos El Patron:** Famous for quesabirria—the cheesy, Tijuana-style beef birria tacos (served with a side of consomé for dipping); be sure not to miss the Taco Patrón, which comes with grilled shrimp and melted cheese.

If all of these tacos have made you thirsty, there are many bars along your route. Of note: Junior at Twenty-Fourth and Utah serves great cocktails in a modern space.

FARMERS MARKET

Almost every neighborhood in San Francisco has a farmers market, sometimes more than once a week. They are low-pressure spots for a first, or fifth, anniversary date spent sampling prepared food and perhaps purchasing a bouquet, but are also great spots for planning a home-cooked dinner together or playing your own version of Iron Chef at home, with each "contestant" selecting two or three must-use ingredients for a combined meal.

- **Ferry Plaza Farmers Market:** You'll see a lot of local chefs at the acclaimed thrice-weekly market. You can come for the produce (come early for the best selection) or for prepared foods, including Primavera Chilaquiles and Roli Roti Porchetta sandwiches. The lunchtime Tuesday and Thursday markets are great spots for a casual lunch date. Saturday: 8:00am – 2:00pm, Tuesday and Thursday lunch.

- **Alemany Farmers Market:** The Alemany Market was the first farmers market in California, opening in 1943. It has been in its current location since 1947.

The only city-run farmers market in San Francisco is bustling and has a reputation for being more affordable, with produce and prepared foods. Saturday, 6:00am - 2:30pm.

- **Heart of the City Farmers Market:** Operating since 1981, Heart of the City is a farmer-operated, nonprofit market that runs year-round in United Nations Plaza. The focus is on supporting and sustaining small farmers and making fresh food more accessible. Sunday 7:00am – 5:00pm; Wednesday: 7:00am–2:00pm.

- **Fort Mason Farmers Market:** Looking for some views with your shopping? The Fort Mason market boasts a view of the bay and bridge, as well as more than 35 vendors. Sunday 9:30am–1:30pm.

- **Outer Sunset Farmers Market and Mercantile:** Farmers, ranchers, music, crafts, and more! This market has some very strong prepared food options, including possibly the best gumbo in town from Gumbo Social. Sunday 9:00am – 3:00pm.

- **Mission Community Market:** Conveniently located Thursday evenings in the Mission, you can shop for dinner or pick up supplies before heading for a drink nearby. Thursday 3:00pm – 7:00pm.

- **Stonestown Market:** As much as it may be amusing to think of a farmers market at a mall, this

Farm Fresh
To You

♥ Ferry Plaza Farmers Market

market is well worth a visit, both for produce and prepared foods. Plus, parking is a breeze. Sundays 9:00am–1:00pm.

BRUNCH

San Francisco loves brunch. It has also been said that San Franciscans love to stand in line for brunch. It seems more likely to be a chicken-or-egg situation in which many of the most popular brunch spots in town do not take reservations, so people have embraced lines. Many places that do not take reservations will allow you to put your name on a list and will give you an estimated wait time. Take the time to stroll the block or visit a neighborhood coffee shop. The recommendations below lean traditional; if you're craving dim sum for brunch, see page 82.

- **Plow:** This Potrero Hill spot is very much not off the radar. Which is a way of saying, expect a long wait. But the best fried potatoes in town, the lemon ricotta pancake of your dreams, and an acclaimed biscuit are well worth your wait. Put your name in, sip some coffee or a mimosa while you wait, or take a stroll to see the killer views of downtown. Pro tip: you can get most of the brunch items on weekdays, when the waits tend to be shorter.

- **Brenda's French Soul Food:** There are now three Brenda's with locations on Divisadero and in Oakland, but this is where it all started. Since 2007 New Orleans native Brenda Buenviaje's food has brought lines of eager diners to the Tenderloin. Not-to-miss items include the very shareable beignet flight, eggs Benedict served on cream biscuits, Shrimp & Grits with Spicy Tomato-Bacon Gravy, and Bananas Foster French Toast.

- **Zazie:** The French bistro in Cole Valley with a charming back patio is a brunch staple thanks to their French toast, "miracle" pancakes, and range of eight benedicts. Unlike many brunch spots which tend to close early, Zazie is also a charming dinner option.

- **Outerlands:** Outerlands serves brunch Thursday through Monday, which is an important thing to remember as peak weekend wait times can be long. Pro tip: Want the food without the wait? Order online for takeout and surprise your special someone with breakfast in bed. The Dutch baby pancake may be slightly less puffy at home, but no one will mind.

- **True Laurel:** Brunch at a bar? With food this good you'll be happy with or without a cocktail. Add an egg to their must-order patty melt or try their grilled cheese and omelet sandwich. Limited brunch reservations are available.

- **Foreign Cinema:** The outdoor patio at Foreign Cinema feels like a celebration any time of day. Oysters and a house-made pop tart are a great way to start before diving into entrees like a Champagne French omelet or a croque monsieur or madame. Plus, reservations are available.

- **Zuni Café:** Can you get the famous roast chicken at brunch? Yes. Can you get the equally famous burger? Yes. But don't miss some of the less-acclaimed items on the menu as well. Reservations available.

- **Rose's Cafe:** This Union Street classic has an extensive brunch menu, but it can be hard to look past the Breakfast Pizza with smoked ham, fontina cheese, and eggs or the Smoked Salmon Pizza with crème fraîche and scrambled eggs. Brunch and weekday breakfast are walk-in only.

- **Front Porch:** Fill up with classic Southern food like chicken and waffles, eggs Benedict, po' boys, and chicken fried steaks. Reservations available.

- **Piccino:** With a light-filled indoor dining area and extensive outdoor space, this Dogpatch charmer features not just acclaimed pizzas at brunch (add an egg!), but also brunch-only treats like savory bread pudding and seasonal scrambles. Reservations available.

- **Balboa Cafe:** This century-old cafe has some of the best outdoor tables for people watching in town. Plus, a Bloody Mary that many feel is worth crossing town for. If you are looking for more of a pick-me-up, don't miss the Balboa Espressotini, now canned in-house so you can take one home after brunch.

- **Auntie April's:** This is a Bayview institution, and after having its fried chicken and waffles (Classic, Cinnamon, or Red Velvet) you will understand why.

- **San Jalisco:** Open for breakfast at 8:00am, this South Van Ness spot has four versions of chilaquiles, breakfast burritos, and weekend specials including Pozole Rojo and Birria en Caldo.

- **El Buen Comer:** This Bernal Heights Mexican spot from an alum of La Cocina features brunch favorites like Chilaquiles and Huevos Divorciados, but the chicken or pork mole are both worth an order. The pozole verde is another highlight.

- **Reem's:** Come to this Mission Street spot to experience the flavors, aromas, and techniques of the modern Arab street corner bakery. Brunch highlights include shakshuka and any of their mana'eesh (flatbreads), especially with an added egg.

FANCY FOR LESS

At last count, San Francisco was the home to around 4,000 restaurants, ranging from takeout only to neighborhood classics to Michelin 3 stars that will awe and amaze. This section focuses on places where you can feel fancy without breaking the bank, whether it is off-menu items at upscale spots or bargain set menus.

- **Hotdog at the Progress:** Sister restaurant to State Bird Provisions and The Anchovy Bar, the Progress has justly received lots of local and national attention. It would be hard to imagine many better-shared dishes than their BBQ Liberty Farms half-duck. But for a much more affordable but equally delightful meal, you can't beat their Prog Dog, double-smoked pork hot dog with bonito-rosemary aioli, kimchi, and toasted sesame on a grilled milk bun paired at the bar with one of their house cocktails.

- **Spruce Burger:** Available on their bar menu, the Spruce Burger is made with a proprietary blend of brisket, short rib, and sirloin, and served on a house-made English muffin. Pair with one of their excellent wines by the glass or cocktails and delight in the attentive service.

- **Trestle:** Trestle offers a nightly changing prix-fixe menu for $39 per person with gracious touches, like soup poured tableside, that make it feel like a steal. Plus, the space is charming.

- **Waterbar:** There are few places in San Francisco with as lovely a view as the Embarcadero's Waterbar. The restaurant focuses on sustainable seafood, and features a full lounge, with views of the Bay Bridge and the Ferry Building. But for bargain hunter purposes, don't miss the $1.55 oyster of the day, available every day.

- **Billingsgate:** This Noe Valley fish market and raw bar offers half-price oysters and cava Tuesdays through Friday from 3:00–5:00pm.

- **Mr. Pollo:** This tiny and dark Mission restaurant serves a 4-course meal for just $40, making it a true bargain. The South American-ish menu starts with a soup or appetizer, followed by the restaurant's signature second-course arepa, a main dish, and dessert.

PRO TIP

Organized by the Golden Gate Restaurant Association, SF Restaurant Week takes place every spring and fall, usually in April and October, and features restaurants across the city offering special menus at set price points for lunch, brunch, and dinner. Prices generally range from $10 to $75, and over 150 venues participate. Oakland, Berkeley, and many other surrounding communities offer their own restaurant weeks throughout the year.

BAKERY TOUR

Some sweets with your sweet? Choose your favorites for a multi-stop tour (croissant crawl, morning bun meander?) or try a bakery of the week for your Sunday morning pastry fix. San Francisco has a bakery, often more than one, in pretty much every neighborhood. Some are destinations, some are more locally focused.

- **B Patisserie:** You are going to be tempted by almost everything at this Pacific Heights bakery with modern French-style pastries along with baked goods inspired by local ingredients. Don't miss the kouign amann, a buttery sugary puff pastry originally from Brittany, perhaps both in original and a seasonal flavor.

- **Tartine:** There are now three Tartines in San Francisco: the original location in the Mission, an Inner Sunset location perfect before or after a trip to the Botanical Gardens, and Tartine Manufactory, which features a full menu in addition to pastries and bread. Highlights include the morning bun, the enormous ham and cheese croissant, bread pudding with seasonal fruit, and the lemon cream tart.

- **Blackjet:** The Bernal Heights bakery that everyone wishes was in their neighborhood. Be sure to try the seasonal Danish on offer, along with the house-made pop tarts and Oreos, and any of the rotating selection of pies. Of note: the holiday-decorated cupcakes—from Pride to Easter to Halloween—are some of the most delightful around.

- **Arsicault:** The lines have not dissipated at their Inner Richmond location since it was declared the "best croissant in America" by *Bon Appétit*. You won't regret waiting, but for a shorter line, try the lesser-known Civic Center location.

- **Breadbelly:** A trio of fine-dining chefs launched this popular Richmond Asian-American bakery. Highlights include kaya toast, a milk bread with coconut-pandan jam, and sandwiches including chicken karaage and char sui.

- **Kantine:** Located in the Castro, Kantine is both a Scandinavian-inspired restaurant and a bakery. You'll want the cinnamon knots and cardamom morning buns, not to mention the pølsehornm, a take on a pig in a blanket.

- **Neighbor Bakehouse:** These croissants include an everything option with poppy and sesame seeds, garlic, green onion, and cream cheese on the inside and a pistachio berry twice-baked version.

- **Jane the Bakery:** With locations in Lower Fillmore, Pacific Heights, and the Tenderloin, Jane serves all manner of breads, breakfast pastries, cakes, and tarts. They have also recently opened Little Jane in

Chinatown, with some items only available there, as well as Toy Boat by Jane, with ice cream. If you are looking for something savory, their sandwiches are recommended.

- **Cinderella:** For more than six decades this Russian baked-goods specialist has been right at home in the Little Russia district of the Richmond. Pierogi, piroshki, and honey cake are highlights.

- **Devil's Teeth:** At their locations in the Outer Sunset and Richmond, you'll want the breakfast sandwich, but also don't miss the cinnamon roll and donut muffins.

- **Bob's Donuts:** Now with a second spot on Baker Street in addition to the original 24-hour location on Polk, Bob's has been family owned and operated since the 1960s. As the name suggests, they specialize in a variety of donuts and pastries including a novelty giant donut. Don't miss the apple fritter.

DIM SUM

Some say you have to head down the Peninsula to find the best dim sum in the area, but there are plenty of spots in town where you can find the dumplings and buns of your dreams. Even in sometimes crowded restaurants, the shared experience can create a sense of intimacy and camaraderie.

▼ Sit-down restaurants

- **Yank Sing:** Open since 1958, Yank Sing is a Michelin Guide Bib Gourmand Restaurant and a winner of a James Beard Foundation America's Classics Award. Which is a way of saying that it is not the cheapest dim sum in town. But it is some of the best and the Rincon Center location, in particular, can feel like an occasion with a very large selection of items on pushcarts wheeled around the restaurant.

- **City View:** Featuring a wide selection of both classic dim sum items and larger entrées, this Chinatown spot sometimes feels like a hidden secret.

- **Dragon Beaux:** Upscale meets Geary Boulevard with a creative dim sum menu that is available both during the day and as part of an extensive dinner menu. You'll see the "Five Guys" xiao long bao on most tables.

- **Palette Tea House:** Dim sum with a view at this Ghirardelli Square spot from the team behind Dragon Beaux and Koi Palace. Be assured that the Instagram-grid-worthy dumplings will taste as good as they look.

- **Hang Ah Tea Room:** This may be the oldest dim sum establishment in the States at more than 100 years old. Keep your eyes peeled for the hand-painted sign at the corner of Sacramento Street Don't forget to get a jar of the chili sauce to take home.

- **Hong Kong Lounge 1:** This Richmond District spot doesn't have carts, but ordering from the menu can be just as fun. Don't miss the baked pork buns or the hard-to-resist Custard Piglet Buns.

- **Harborview:** With views of the Ferry Building and the Bay Bridge, Harborview has one of the most scenic patios along the Embarcadero.

- **Dumpling Alley:** A neighborhood staple between the Presidio and Lincoln Park, this spot is well worth a visit for a wide selection of boiled dumplings (available in both cooked and frozen versions).

- **Yuanbao Jiaozi:** Yuanbao Jiaozi is all about the dumplings, freshly made by hand, boiled, and served straight-up or in soup.

- **Dumpling Specialist:** This small restaurant has a limited menu focused on classic boiled dumplings. Also don't skip the pan-fried pork buns and wonton soup.

Takeout

- **Takeout dim sum has advantages:** you can eat at a nearby park or take your treats home. The disadvantage: you may struggle to not tear into your favorites on the way!

- **Good Mong Kok:** This Chinatown bakery has mastered the art of takeout dim sum. There will be a line, but it generally moves quickly. The char siu bao is a highlight.

- **Dim Sum Bistro:** Also in Chinatown and open daily from 9:00am, try the turnip cakes, pork buns, and the wide range of rice rolls.

- **Wing Sing:** This Chinatown spot offers all of the standards, but you'll see most everyone ordering one of their large and fully stuffed chicken buns.

- **Good Luck Dim Sum:** This classic Clement Street standout is both speedy and affordable, as well as cash only. It is a great pre–Golden Gate Park stop.

- **Lung Fung Bakery:** This Clement Street spot has some of the best pork buns in town.

- **Asian American Food Company/Kingdom of Dumpling:** This frozen dumpling shop, affiliated with the nearby restaurant, sells a large selection of dumplings plus frozen xiao long bao (soup dumplings) and other dough-based specialties. Stock your freezer for at-home dumplings by candlelight.

FERRY BUILDING

Both a working transportation hub and an artisan food marketplace, this historic landmark and home of the city's best-known farmers market (see page 68) is a must-do for visitors and a regular destination for many locals. The 245-foot-tall clock tower is modeled after the clock tower of the Giralda Cathedral in Seville, Spain, and an iconic piece of San Francisco's skyline. The building also hosts numerous events, including a flea market, live music, and an array of seasonal activities. There are many ways to experience the Ferry Building. You can enjoy a sit-down meal or wander the food hall, picking items to enjoy in the outdoor seating or to take home for a feast.

▼ Restaurants

- **Gott's: Bay Area comfort food at its finest:** classic and creative cheeseburgers, incredible onion rings, shakes and wine alongside ahi poke tacos, fresh salads, and seasonal specials, including a crab roll.

- **Hog Island Oyster Company:** Hog Island Oyster Company is an oyster bar, full-service bar, restaurant, and retail outlet from the Tomales Bay oyster farm of the same name. A seat at the bar provides a great water view—through floor-to-ceiling windows looking out on the San Francisco Bay. And,

of course, the oysters are impeccably fresh, plus there's a stellar grilled cheese.

- **Slanted Door:** Charles Phan's nationally acclaimed Vietnamese restaurant not only has excellent food, but a wall of floor-to-ceiling windows that overlook the bay in the contemporary, open-space design.

- **Grande Creperie:** It's like being in France when you taste these naturally leavened-style crêpes and artisanal all-butter croissants and pastries.

- **Señor Sisig:** Launched as a food truck in 2010, Señor Sisig eventually opened brick-and-mortar locations, including in the Mission. This location features all of the restaurant's greatest hits (burritos,

♥ Hog Island Oyster Company

tacos, and nachos with Filipino flavors), with the welcome addition of cocktails.

- **Delica:** A Japanese delicatessen with a world cuisine menu, you can pick up a bento lunch or dinner with an assortment of the day, or choose a la carte items.

- **Reem's California:** This beloved Arab bakery from renowned chef Reem Assil is a great spot to pick up flatbreads covered in za'atar, house-made dips, and fresh-baked pastries.

Food Hall Vendors

- **Acme Bakery:** The Ferry Building Marketplace is the only place in the Bay Area—other than Acme's original Berkeley location—that carries the full selection of Acme's artisan breads, along with pastries and other specialty items.

- **Ferry Plaza Wine Merchant:** In the style of European wine merchants, this is a classic, hands-on, service-oriented shop for buying, tasting, and learning about wine. Their Wednesday Flight Nights are a great chance to taste celebrated wines and meet the people who make them.

- **Fort Point:** Fort Point's North Arcade kiosk is a place for customers to enjoy brewery-fresh beer on-site or packaged to take home.

LA COCINA MUNICIPAL MARKETPLACE

For a different food hall experience, don't miss La Cocina Municipal Marketplace. Named by the *San Francisco Chronicle* as one of the Top 25 Restaurants in the Bay Area in 2022, the marketplace is not just a delicious place to eat, it stands as an innovative model of conscious, community-led development that offers economic opportunity for women entrepreneurs, jobs for Tenderloin residents, and a welcoming and affordable dining space for community members and those looking to eat with purpose.

- **Miette Patisserie:** The pale pink walls and lovingly created cakes, cookies, and pastries in the glass display cases evoke a slice of Parisian life on the San Francisco Bay. The cupcakes are hard to resist.

- **Red Bay:** Stop by and experience their signature Charcoal Vanilla Latte, Candied Yam Latte, and the new line of ready-to-drink Black Coffee Spritzers.

- **Far West Fungi:** A one-stop destination for mushrooms, this shop carries a wide selection of culinary mushrooms (both fresh and dried), medicinal mushroom supplements, and even mushroom logs to grow your own at home.

- **Recchiuti Confections:** The Paris-inspired, locally made company is nationally renowned for its full line of fine chocolates. There are weekly specials, seasonal and holiday selections, and confections that are available nowhere else.

- **Imperial Tea Court:** Renowned as an exclusive source for many of the most sought-after teas produced today, Imperial Tea Court carries over 100 teas, including organic varieties, and a beautiful selection of tea pots, many of which are handmade by masters in China. Visitors can purchase tea or pause for tea and snacks.

MAKE A LIST

No matter where you live, you've seen the lists. Whether it is fried chicken or banh mi or donuts, there are recommended "best of" lists available for most everything you can think of! Now it is time to make your own.

How? Start with the question, or questions: What is your favorite food? Your partner's? The first meal you ate together? The place you have always wanted to try? Those are all good starting points.

Once you've chosen your item of focus, it is time for some research. Consulting lists from local food writers, asking friends, and keeping your eyes open on your walks are all good starting points. Think about a blend of neighborhood favorites, highly reviewed spots, and maybe a few you are simply curious about.

Is your list ready? It is time to think about how you would like to attack it. Is this an item that makes sense for a crawl? Think smaller items you can eat numerous tastes of in one day. Or is it best for a weekly quest? Think fried chicken Fridays, pasta Sunday suppers, French fry Thursdays, etc.

Here's a sample list for burgers, for inspiration.

♥ Neighborhood Favorites

- **Beep's Burgers:** Since 1962, Beep's has been serving burgers, milkshakes, fries, and more on Ocean Avenue. Named after the signature "beep" of the Space Age satellites, this is a throwback drive-in with a modern take, serving 100% Angus beef and focusing on fresh, local ingredients.

- **Sam's:** Since 1966, this Anthony Bourdain-approved spot has been serving late-night burgers, perfect for a post-event fix.

- **Red's Java House:** Perched on the corner of Pier 30, Red's has served the city its famous sourdough cheeseburgers and inexpensive beer since 1955. Once called "the Chartres Cathedral of cheap eats" by longtime Chronicle writer Carl Nolte.

- **Wesburger 'n' More:** Classic and creative burgers along with excellent fried chicken and great tater tots in the Mission.

- **4505 Meats:** Why, yes, they do call their burger "The Best Damn Grass-Fed Cheeseburger." After trying the quarter-pound patty with lettuce, onion, Gruyere cheese, and secret sauce on a buttery, griddled sesame and scallion bun, you may agree.

Fancier

- **Nopa:** Wood-grilled, served with spectacular fries, and eaten at the bar with an excellent cocktail, you'll not only be in love with your date, but with San Francisco too.

- **Causwells:** This Chestnut Street bistro makes a bold claim on its website: "Our smash-style Americana Cheeseburger is beloved, some say it's the best in the country."

- **Wayfare Tavern:** The fried chicken gets a lot of attention, but the Tavern burger—proprietary grind of beef, Marin brie, red onion marmalade, and smoked bacon on a brioche bun—is a great choice.

- **Spruce:** Available on their bar menu, the Spruce burger is made with a house blend of brisket, short rib, and sirloin, and served on a house-made English muffin. Pair with one of their excellent wines by the glass or cocktail.

- **ABV:** A great bar, with a great burger, that is often recommended as a first-date spot, because you can start with drinks and if things are going well, move on to food. But don't let that stop you from going for your fifth or fiftieth date.

- **Monsieur Benjamin:** Sure, you could enjoy any of the French classics at the Hayes Valley Bistro, but don't overlook the charcoal-grilled hamburger, fully dressed with Comté cheese and served with impeccable fries. The fries paired with a cocktail at the bar are also an excellent choice.

- **Mission Bowling Club:** Whether or not you are interested in bowling, it is worth a trip for the burger, made with organic beef, Monterey jack, caramelized onion, and caper aioli on an Acme pain de mie bun.

CLASSIC SAN FRANCISCO

Sometimes you want to feel like you are in a classic film. That could be dressing up to sip cocktails in a room that your grandparents might recognize, or heading somewhere that feels so much a part of the city that everyone knows its name. San Francisco is lucky to have a range of spots that fit the bill for when you are feeling fancy or simply embracing classic comfort.

- **House of Prime Rib:** Since 1949, the House of Prime Rib has been a place to celebrate birthdays, family get-togethers, or simply having made it through another week. Although there are other options, you are here for their house salad, dressed at the table; prime rib, carved from silver zeppelins; and the accompaniments, preferably served with an ice-cold martini or Manhattan. Pro tip: reservations book up months in advance, but walking in for a seat at the bar is a worthwhile option.

- **Original Joe's:** With locations in North Beach and just over the Daly City border in Westlake, Original Joe's dates back to 1937. You are here, hopefully in a booth, to enjoy classic Italian American fare like veal or eggplant parmigiana, arancini, Joe's famous hamburger (laced with onions in a sourdough roll), or the classic Joe's special: a signature scramble of ground beef, spinach, onions, and eggs.

- **Gold Mirror:** Tucked away in Inner Parkside since 1969, Gold Mirror is a family-owned neighborhood gem that makes you feel like a regular even on your first visit. Have a calamari steak, the chicken piccata, or the house-made cannelloni and enjoy the old-school service.

- **Tadich Grill:** Opened in 1849 as a coffee stand, Tadich Grill is California's oldest operating restaurant and the third oldest in the US. Order the cioppino or sand dabs and a classic cocktail.

- **Sam's Grill:** Sam's has served fresh fish and classic San Francisco dishes since 1867. You won't go wrong with any of their mesquite grille fish, but since we are here for the classics, why not Celery Victor or Hangtown Fry? Request a private booth with a curtain, for a truly old-school experience.

- **John's Grill:** As mentioned in *The Maltese Falcon*, the wood-paneled walls of John's Grill will transport you to an earlier era. Order petrale sole, chicken Jerusalem, or the Sam Spade special (chops, baked potato, sliced tomato).

- **Old Clam House:** The Old Clam House has been in the same location since 1861. Celebrate its longevity with clams of all kinds, from clam cioppino, to clams gratinate, clam chowder, and clams linguine.

- **Tosca:** Stop by for a nightcap at this bar and

restaurant originally opened in November 1919. You'll want a seat at the long bar to enjoy the house "cappuccino" (hot chocolate and steamed milk with brandy).

- **Sam Wo:** The self-proclaimed "oldest restaurant in Chinatown" was built after the 1906 earthquake. It closed in 2021 before reopening in its current location.

- **Red's Java House:** Perched on the corner of Pier 30, Red's has served the city its famous sourdough cheeseburgers and inexpensive beer since 1955. Dubbed "the Chartres Cathedral of cheap eats" by long time *Chronicle* writer Carl Nolte.

OF NOTE

There are several other classics sprinkled through the book including the Balboa (see page 76), The Buena Vista café (see page 144), and Hang Ah Tea Room (see page 83).

- **Tommy's Joynt:** Open since 1947, Tommy's is a destination for carved-to-order hot pastrami sandwiches, an impressive selection of beers, and is one of the rare places open until midnight on weekends.

- **Fior D'Italia:** First established in 1886 in the heart of North Beach, this is America's oldest Italian restaurant still in operation. Order classics such as fried calamari, Caesar salad, osso buco with polenta, or homemade pastas.

- **Schroeder's:** Founded in 1893, Schroeder's is a Bavarian-inspired beer hall. Have some tots or schnitzel and imagine yourself on vacation.

- **Swan Oyster Depot:** Expect a line at this tiny oyster bar, open since 1912. It's all great—the chowder, Louie salads, seafood cocktails, fresh oysters—but don't miss the Sicilian sashimi: thinly sliced raw fish with a drizzle of olive oil, black pepper, and capers.

Maybe any restaurant can be romantic with the right companion. But the spots below regularly make the lists of most romantic in the city, so count on them to set the right mood. Note: some of these spots are close to splurge territory. See guidance on how to stay under or at least close to budget.

- **Cafe Jacqueline:** For more than 40 years, this North Beach spot has focused on souffles. You can start with onion soup, but sharing a savory followed by a sweet souffle is the right move. One thing to know: meals tend to be leisurely, so clear your schedule for the evening. Also, reservations are essential, and by phone only.

- **Bix:** Bix feels like a 1930s supper club, with excellent cocktails and live music every night. This is a spot to dress up. Reserve for dinner or sit at the bar for cocktails and appetizers.

- **The Matterhorn:** Even if you are not seated in the gondola for two, sharing a bubbling cheese fondue is a warm and romantic way to spend a foggy evening.

- **Foreign Cinema:** Highlighted in the brunch section (see page 72), at night you can watch subtitled films on the back wall of their courtyard under heat lamps and twinkling string lights.

- **Cotogna:** Dine beneath olive trees with fairy lights and heat lamps to keep you nice and toasty in arguably the city's prettiest parklet. You won't go wrong sharing a pizza and a pasta or two.

- **Empress by Boon:** One of the few places in town with a dress code, Empress by Boon offers a not-inexpensive prix fixe menu, with hard-to-get reservations. But you can walk into the bar and lounge and order a la carte.

- **Boulevard:** This beautiful restaurant is housed in one of the few buildings downtown to have survived the 1906 earthquake. Although sitting in the dining room may be over budget, you can enjoy drinks and food a la carte in the bar area.

- **Penny Roma:** This dimly lit and plant-filled courtyard, with a retractable roof from the team behind Flour & Water, is perfect for sharing crudo and pasta.

- **Waterbar/Epic Steak:** Come to these sister restaurants for stunning up-close views of the waterfront and the Bay Bridge lights. To cut down on costs, try the bar menu at Waterbar or brunch at Epic Steak.

- **Nari:** Infusing heritage Thai recipes with a modern Californian sensibility, Nari is an exceptional restaurant for adventurous eating and sharing. For a more affordable option, the bar and lounge are available for a la carte dining.

EAT OUTSIDE

One of the bright spots of the Covid pandemic was the explosion of outdoor dining options due to the city's Shared Spaces program. Instituted as a temporary measure when indoor dining was closed, this program has been made permanent, which means that many of the outdoor "parklets" will remain intact or with minor changes.

The city has reported over 1,000 Shared Spaces locations in neighborhoods across the city. Although not all of them are restaurants, that number gives a sense of just how many new options exist. Most have heat lamps, so they are options nearly year-round.

- **State Bird Provisions:** State Bird's modern "dim sum" on traditional carts and trays makes it a fun eating experience. Their outdoor area with wooden floors, art-covered walls, and ample plants takes that energy outdoors. Plus, additional seats make it slightly easier to get a reservation.

- **Rintaro:** The plant-filled and tree-shaded courtyard makes this restaurant feel like an escape. Like the space, the small plates such as sashimi and yakitori may be the best izakaya dishes in the city.

- **Mission Rock Resort:** Feast on oysters and fish-and-chips on the waterfront patio located on the

shores of Mission Bay and down the street from the Chase Center.

- **Hook Fish Co:** This Outer Sunset sustainable fish restaurant and market has a handsome wooden parklet out front for on-site outdoor dining, perfect for enjoying fish-and-chips or fish tacos near the beach.

- **Prubechu:** Taking over the parking lot alongside its building created a big patio setup, perfect for the occasional pig roast. The only restaurant in San Francisco spotlighting the cuisine of the indigenous peoples of Guam and the Marianas Islands, the food is a mix of traditional Chamorro dishes with Spanish, Japanese, and American influences.

- **Blue Plate:** This neighborhood go-to has a back patio that has been an outdoor favorite for years.

Whether you go for the fried chicken, classic meatloaf, or an assortment of small plates, you won't want to miss a dessert slice of key lime pie.

- **All Good Pizza:** An outdoor pizza and beer and wine garden located in the often sunny Bayview is hard to resist.

- **Chuy's Fiestas:** Stop in at this Mission Mexican spot for shrimp tacos and aguachile verde in their enclosed backyard patio.

- **The Ramp:** Originally a public boat ramp and bait shop in the 1950s, The Ramp is situated on the water's edge in Dogpatch. Brunch is particularly popular, and The Ramp amusingly has been included both on best places to go on a date and best places to break up lists.

- **The Vault Garden:** A temperature-controlled, weather-protected, socially safe dining environment—which is a fancy way of saying, very well tented. Located downtown, it has lounge seating for relaxed cocktails as well as an all-day menu for full meals.

- **The Anchovy Bar:** A bit of a splurge, but eating local anchovies, oysters, and the chips and dip of your dreams is worth some advance planning. Don't miss the Western Addition Oyster: two broiled oysters with smoky date-bacon sambal butter.

GET OUT OF TOWN

Getting out of the city can be a nice change of pace. In this section you'll find some of the best nearby getaways, from coastal restaurants to ferry rides and hikes. "Nearby" is the key word here, so no Napa, Sonoma, Santa Cruz, Tahoe, or Yosemite. But yes to Alameda, Berkeley, Sausalito, Oakland, and Half Moon Bay. Plus, a night tour of Alcatraz and a trip to a beach that makes you feel like you've left the city!

♥ Bixby Creek Bridge

SAUSALITO

The wind in your hair. Alcatraz to your right, the Pacific Ocean to your left. There is a reason that a walk or bike ride across the Golden Gate Bridge is a draw for visitors and locals. If you do not have a bike, there are numerous rental options, including at Fisherman's Wharf or at Sports Basement in the Presidio. The approximate duration and distance from Fisherman's Wharf to Sausalito is ninety minutes / 8 miles, slightly shorter from the Presidio. The advantage of renting from the wharf is that the return ferry will arrive there.

The ferry terminal in Sausalito is on the northern end of downtown. Blue & Gold Fleet offers a regular ferry service between Sausalito and San Francisco. If you don't bike, the ferry both ways is a great option. Alternatively, you can drive or take a rideshare.

♥ Eat & Drink

- **Fish:** Order at the counter and sit at an outdoor picnic table beside the harbor to enjoy a generous portion of whatever's fresh.

- **Equator Coffee:** If you are looking for a pick-me-up after your ride, don't miss the Shakerato: two espresso shots, dark brown sugar, and heavy cream shaken until frothy.

- **Le Garage:** For a taste of France in Sausalito, this former garage with indoor-outdoor seating is a charmer.

- **Joinery:** Order in the front, take a number, and grab a seat to enjoy seasonal fare and views of the bay from the dock out back.

- **Bar Bocce:** Fire pits and a bocce court and pizza? It is not surprising that this is a very popular date spot, with or without the bridge ride.

- **Bump Bar:** Feeling fancy? This small bar and cafe offers sustainably sourced caviar and roe and other seafood-focused items.

- **Poggio:** Northern Italian comfort food meets comfy old-world interiors at this well-loved trattoria that is well known for their negronis.

- **Copita:** The menu is 100 percent gluten-free, and the tequila bar serves over 100 varieties. The bar and outdoor patio are great for people watching.

MUIR WOODS

Walking through a forest of old-growth coast redwoods is not just for out-of-towners. You can do Muir Woods like the tourists and stay on the boardwalk or you can venture off the beaten path on trails that will bring solitude and the perfect place to feel alone, together.

- **Getting there:** Muir Woods was once a first-come, first-served parking situation. Those days are long gone with parking reservations now required. For those unable to get a reservation or without a car, there is a shuttle service available from both the Larkspur and Sausalito ferry stations. Advance tickets are recommended.

- **Hiking:** Muir Woods National Monument contains 6 miles of trails. There are also longer hikes on trails that extend into surrounding Mount Tamalpais State Park, so you will have choices to make. The trails on the forest floor are asphalt or boardwalk whereas the trails on the canyon walls are dirt, narrow, steep, and rutted with tree roots. The forest changes with the seasons, so expect babbling brooks and deep greens during the winter and dryer conditions in the summer and fall.

Because the trails vary in distance and difficulty and cell phone access is intermittent at Muir Woods, it is strongly advised to

OF NOTE

Muir Woods is, obviously, a living national monument, which means that it changes through the seasons and trails open and close, so be sure to check the website before heading out. Also, please obey the posted signs about staying on the trails to protect the delicate forest ecosystem.

♥ Muir Woods

research ahead of time if you are looking to do any of the more challenging trails.

The main trail begins at the visitor center and follows Redwood Creek on both sides of the stream. You can enjoy views of old-growth redwood forest from a stroller and wheelchair-accessible boardwalk.

- **Fern Creek to Camp Alice Eastwood Loop:** Hike along lush Fern Creek through a redwood canyon. After following the creek you'll climb uphill toward Camp Alice Eastwood where you'll find water, restrooms, and picnic tables. The Plevin Cut Trail, originally part of an early-1900s rail line, will lead you back to Muir Woods' main trail via Camp Eastwood Trail.

- The Ben Johnson Trail takes you through a tree-shaded canyon filled with majestic redwoods and eventually opens up to immaculate views of San Francisco, the sparkling sea, and nearby hills.

- **The Dipsea Trail:** Leave the main area of Muir Woods and climb to a view of Mt. Tamalpais, San Francisco, and the Pacific Ocean.

- **Bootjack Trail:** This is a favorite during the rainy season, as you will pass numerous waterfalls large and small. The main trail becomes the Bootjack Trail after you pass bridge 4. You can walk as far as you like, circle back, and do a loop with a connecting trail.

Eat & Drink

Although there is limited food available at Muir Woods, here are a few suggestions for places to stop for a bite on your way back to the city.

- **Pelican Inn:** Stop for a ploughman's lunch or fish-and-chips at this Muir Beach British-themed inn.

- **Buckeye Roadhouse:** Open since 1937, this Marin classic is an easy stop on your way back to the Golden Gate Bridge. Open for lunch and dinner on weekends and dinner only during the week, you can make reservations for the alpine-lodge-style dining room or walk in for seats at the bar. Try comfort food items like Oysters Bingo, baby back ribs, and brick chicken.

- **Hook Fish Co:** Come to this counter-service spot for some of the best seafood around. Like its San Francisco location, you won't go wrong with poke, fish tacos, or fish-and-chips. Plus, the adjacent Proof Lab will provide just the beer you are looking for.

- **Sol Food:** This Marin favorite serves Puerto Rican cuisine, including Creole prawns, mofongo, maduros and tostones, and a chuleton sandwich on French bread.

- **The Junction Beer Garden and Bottle Shop:** A tap room and bottle shop with pizza.

ALAMEDA

A day trip that includes one of the best views of the San Francisco skyline? A closer look at the port of Oakland? A visit to a town so close to San Francisco that still feels like a getaway? Then the Alameda Ferry is for you!

You can catch the Alameda Ferry at the Ferry Building. If you have a bike, that is a great way to get around Alameda. If not, many activities are centered in a few locations, so rideshares are also a good option.

- **Alameda Point:** The (free) Spirits Alley Trolley travels between the Alameda-Main Street and Seaplane Lagoon ferry terminals, making multiple stops along the route at the distilleries, breweries, and wineries. The trolley operates on Fridays from 4-10pm and Saturdays and Sundays from 1-7pm.

OF NOTE

The last ferry back to San Francisco is 8:55pm on weekends, and 9:55pm on weekdays, so plan this as a day trip or be prepared for an early dinner.

- **Hangar 1:** Housed in an old WWII aircraft hangar, a trip to Hangar 1 provides a chance to taste their vodkas straight, in cocktails, or paired with caviar or cheese. The distillery tour is a great way to learn more about the process. Be sure to bring home a bottle or two to relive your day with cocktails at home!

- **Faction Brewing:** Beer with a view. This tasting room features unobstructed views of the San Francisco skyline and Bay Bridge, plus over twenty beers on draft. There is both indoor and outdoor seating available. There are also frequent visits from local food trucks to satisfy your snacking needs.

- **The Rake at Admiral Maltings:** Adjacent to the brewing facility, this pub offers cold beer, snacks, and sandwiches.

- **Almanac Barrel House, Brewery, and Taproom:** Great beer, food trucks, and special events like beer yoga. Their beers span the gamut from delicate oak-aged lagers to nuanced barrel-aged sours, decadent stouts, and hazy IPAs, so there is something to make everyone happy.

- **Pacific Pinball Museum:** Bring back memories or make new ones at this interactive museum that offers ninety playable pinball machines that span decades. Unlimited play with admission.

THE ALAMEDA POINT ANTIQUES FAIRE

This is the largest antiques show in Northern California. Held on the first Sunday of every month, the Faire boasts over 800 dealer booths. All items are 20 years old or older, and items include vintage and antique home decorations, clothing, furniture, and art.

And don't miss the nearby East Ocean Seafood, with Hong-Kong-style dim sum served at lunch, featuring a huge selection of dishes served on the traditional carts.

▼ Downtown/Park Street

The main drag in Alameda is a great place to stroll and dip into and out of shops. While you walk, you may want to follow along with the Historic Self-Guided Walking Tour: downtownalameda.com/about/history/

- **Alameda Theater and Cineplex:** This fully restored Art Deco movie theater built in 1932 now has multiple screens for classic and new-release films.

Eat & Drink

- Farmstead Cheeses and Wines is the destination for all of your picnic needs and has been named Best Cheese Store and Best Wine Store by several East Bay publications.

- **Julie's Coffee and Tea Garden:** More than 20 kinds of tea along with coffee, baked goods, and organic meals in a charming setting make for a delightful stop.

- **Crispian Bakery:** Breakfast pastries are a highlight on this menu of French-inspired American breads and pastry.

- **Spinning Bones:** California rotisserie-roasted meats with bold Hawaiian and Japanese flavors, and the burger is one of the best around.

- **Wild Ginger:** Spicy cold noodles and dumplings are some of the highlights from this Xi'an-style street food spot that offers indoor and outdoor dining.

- **Sandwich Board:** Although there are plenty of options, you are here for the in-house roasted turkey, preferably on Dutch crunch.

- **Alley and Vine:** Seasonal and locally sourced food with excellent cocktails, open for both dinner and weekend brunch.

- **Ole's Waffle Shop:** Established in 1927, Ole's Waffle is a neighborhood diner serving up famous pancakes and waffles, and the perfect place to imagine yourself as an extra in *Happy Days*.

GRAY WHALE COVE

You will need a car for this one, but it is worth it! Just minutes south of the city, you will find yourself driving along the sort of California coastline seen in the movies.

You can and should stop at any of the beaches that catch your eye between Pacifica and Half Moon Bay, but Gray Whale Cove and the easy hike along the hillside above is your destination. The hike takes you above Highway 1 between Montara State Beach and Gray Whale Cove and is approximately one mile each way with an elevation change of only 130 feet. Take in the wildflowers, crashing waves, and, if you are lucky, spot a bunny along the trail. If you have brought a picnic, there are several benches with views, or you can descend to the beaches on either end for a shoreside meal.

PACIFICA

Eat & Drink

- **Rosalind Bakery:** A great place to stop on the way for pastries, bread to take home, and sandwiches, including a breakfast sandwich with pimento cheese. The cinnamon roll is a particular delight.

- **Mazzetti's Bakery:** You may feel like you have stepped back in time to the bakeries of childhood at this long-running family-owned Italian bakery that specializes in cakes, donuts, and focaccia. The Derby Cake is a celebration-in-a-box with chocolate and vanilla sponge, whipped cream, and fresh strawberries and bananas.

- **Gorilla Barbeque:** A takeout BBQ restaurant in a converted rail car. Try the brisket or ribs with a side of corn bread.

♥ Gray Whale Cove

- **Nick's:** This old-school joint with a view of Rockaway Beach has one of the best crab sandwiches around. The crab Benedict is another highlight.

HALF MOON BAY

Continue driving south down Highway 1 after your hike and you will reach Half Moon Bay. Perhaps most famous for its Pumpkin Festival and the weighing of pumpkins as big as some cars, it is also a great destination for a post-hike meal.

TACO BELL

Yes, really. The Taco Bell in Pacifica has been called the world's most beautiful Taco Bell. Now that may sound like faint praise, but, really, how many fast food restaurants can you whale watch from? Plus, this Taco Bell has alcoholic drinks. Whether you love or hate Taco Bell, this location is a great place to stop for an Instagram-worthy photo.

▼ Eat & Drink

- **Dad's Luncheonette:** Nationally acclaimed burgers and mushroom sandwiches from a former fine-dining chef served from an old caboose. The hours are limited and the waits can be long, but you won't regret it.

- **Sam's Chowder House:** A lobster roll on the deck at Sam's has been called a quintessential Half Moon

Bay experience. Take in the views at this casual seafood experience reminiscent of an East Coast-style seafood shack.

- **Hop Dogma Brewing Company:** Craft beers in seaside digs with a welcoming vibe.

- **La Costanera:** A contemporary, authentic Peruvian restaurant overlooking the ocean with a menu that highlights the coastal cuisine of Latin America and has an extensive cocktail list. Try the cebiche tasting to share.

- **Half Moon Bay Brewing:** One of the oldest breweries on the coast offers a big patio with fire pits, local beers, and tempting dishes, including Avo's Portuguese Fisherman's Stew, a family recipe created by co-founder and owner Lenny Mendonca's "Avo."

OAKLAND

Like San Francisco, Oakland is a city of neighborhoods. It is also, on either BART or the Bay Bridge, easy to get to from much of San Francisco, so for many it is a regular stop for dinner, drinks, a show, or more. Plus, it is often warmer and sunnier than San Francisco. You'll see Oakland spots sprinkled through other entries, but here are a few specific neighborhoods for a more focused

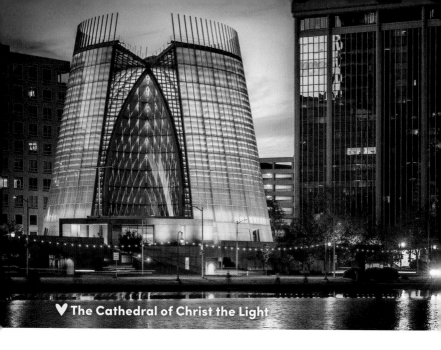

♥ The Cathedral of Christ the Light

visit. One could write a whole book of dates focused on this city, so additional exploration is highly recommended, especially as some favorite spots fall outside of the neighborhoods below.

DOWNTOWN AND UPTOWN:

Downtown refers to the area on Broadway from 8th to 17th Streets, whereas Uptown is Broadway and Telegraph, between 17th and 25th Streets. You may also think of this area as near the Fox and Paramount theaters.

♥ Eat & Drink

Alamar Kitchen and Sobre Mesa: Both of these

restaurants are from Chef Nelson German, who you may remember from *Top Chef* Season 18. Alamar Kitchen is seafood focused and you'd be wise to try a crab or shrimp boil to share. Sobre Mesa is an Afro-Latino spot, featuring lush surroundings, refined cocktails, seasonal cuisine, and up-tempo music. Don't miss their namesake cocktail.

- **Cafe Van Cleef:** Open since 2004 and located just one block from the Fox Theater, Cafe Van Kleef is known for its greyhounds with fresh-squeezed grapefruit juice.

- **Friends & Family:** Recently named one of the 50 best bars in North America, this women-led bar serves excellent food and craft cocktails in an inclusive, queer-friendly space. Of note, the bar features a "daily affirmations" monthly shot special, where 100 percent of the proceeds go to gender-affirming surgery fundraising efforts. If it is on the menu, don't miss Mom's Carrot Cake.

- **Palmetto:** A Caribbean-inspired destination from the owners of the Kon-Tiki cocktail bar nearby.

- **Kingston 11:** Come for Jamaican and Californian cuisines using local and organic ingredients. Stay for the music and vibe. Don't miss the salt cod fritters and oxtail stew.

- **Viridian:** Savory small dishes and unique desserts

inspired by the Asian American experience, paired with gorgeous cocktails.

- **Shawarmaji:** This Jordanian-style chicken shawarma shop serves halal meat wraps, loaded fries, and salads. In 2021 it was included on *Esquire* magazine's Best New Restaurants in America list.

- **Hopscotch:** American regional classics influenced by Japanese flavors and techniques. Along with dinner, weekend brunch is a highlight.

- **Duende:** At this Spanish spot from Chef Paul Canales be sure to order the cabbage salad that has a fan club and any of their paellas, including the fideua, which substitutes pasta for the traditional rice.

- **Lion Dance Cafe:** This vegan restaurant is inspired by Singaporean hawker fare, Chinese-Singaporean family recipes, and more. The shaobing sandwich was named Best in the Bay by the *San Francisco Chronicle*.

- **Mela Bistro:** This modern Ethiopian bistro is a charmer with a seasonal vegetarian platter, asa wot (fish goulash), and chicken tibs (free-range chicken breast cubes, sautéed with onions, garlic, ginger, jalapeños, and clarified butter and herbs).

- **Aburaya:** A punk rock–themed Japanese fried chicken restaurant could be just the thing before a show.

- **Drake's Dealership:** This open-air beer garden with 32 beers on tap and wood-fired pizza is rarely a bad idea.

- **Slug Bar:** From the team behind Snail Bar, Slug is a natural wine bar and bottle stocked with a curated menu and wine selection that changes with the season.

- **Lovely's:** The burgers and chicken sandwiches are both stellar, but don't look past the fried fish sandwich.

FRUITVALE

The main strip is International Boulevard, which lives up to its name, though there is an undeniable emphasis on Latin America. There is a BART stop right in the heart of things.

Eat & Drink

- **Guadalajara Restaurant & Tequila Bar:** You won't be disappointed by the tacos, but they also serve some of the best and largest burritos in the area.

- **Aguachiles El Tamarindo:** The colorful Sinaloan truck has a long menu of aguachiles, ceviches, and seafood towers. They also have excellent birria tacos.

- **La Grana Fish:** Try the quesabirria—tacos topped

with cheese and slow-braised beef, then griddled until crisp on the flat-top.

- **Mariscos La Costa:** As the name suggests, excellent seafood. Highlights include seafood cocktail and ceviche.

- **Tacos El Último Baile:** This acclaimed taco truck is transitioning to a permanent space inside the Fruitvale Public Market where they will serve Northern Mexico–style tacos using mesquite charcoal, handmade flour tortillas, and simple street-style ingredients made from scratch.

- **El Huarache Azteca:** Family-run since 2001, this has long been a top destination for the food of Mexico City—especially for its namesake huaraches (sandal-shaped fried masa cakes), sopes, and other masa-based dishes.

- **Nieves Cinco de Mayo:** Family-owned and run, Nieves Cinco De Mayo specializes in home made churned ice cream. Using only natural fruits, milk, and sugar, and no heavy creams, they have a wide range of ice creams and sorbets to choose from. Mangonada is particularly popular.

- **Churros Mexicanos:** Crispy churros, made to order and filled with smooth custard, are a perfect sweet treat.

- **Lucky Three Seven:** This East Oakland mainstay is

♥ Oakland's Lake Merritt

the spot for lumpia; meaty, slow-cooked Filipino stews; and chicken wings.

- **Banh Mi Ba Le:** The gold standard for banh mi in the East Bay, with some of the best bread around. The lines may be long, but they move quickly. A true bargain.

- **Wahpepah's Kitchen:** Come to this restaurant to explore indigenous ingredients in dishes that celebrate native cuisine, including bison blue-corn tacos, deer sticks, and macron crepes.

- **El Paisa@.com:** The truly terrible name can be forgiven for the truly wonderful tacos. For more adventurous types, the tripe is a highlight. Those less adventurous can try the suadero. Don't miss the excellent salsa selection.

- **Red Bay Coffee Headquarters Cafe:** Founded in 2014 by Keba Konte, Red Bay Coffee, is, in their words: "at the forefront of what we believe is the fourth wave of coffee—a firm commitment to ensure coffee production is not only high quality and sustainable, but a vehicle for diversity, inclusion, social and economic restoration, entrepreneurship, and environmental sustainability." Which is a long way of saying, good people doing good while making excellent coffee. Have a drink here and don't forget a bag to enjoy at home.

ROCKRIDGE/TEMESCAL:

Centered around College Avenue and Telegraph Avenue (between 40th and 51st).

Eat & Drink

- **Yimm Oakland:** With a focus on Thai home cooking, Yimm is a great place for dishes like Mee Cook (Grandma's recipe!) or Tom Yum Omelet Rice (organic free-range eggs* with milk, Tom Yum shrimp, oyster mushroom, Kaffir lime leaves, served over rice).

- **Belotti:** This small Rockridge spot has been called the king of fresh pasta in the East Bay. You won't go wrong with any of the pastas but a highlight is the Agnolotti (traditional Piedmontese-style stuffed

GRAND LAKE/LAKE MERRITT

Centered around Grand and Lakeshore Avenues, this neighborhood features a wonderful classic movie theater, one of the best farmers markets in the area, a delightful rose garden, and many bars and restaurants. Plus, the Oakland Museum of California has collections of art, history, and natural science that bring to life first-person accounts and often untold narratives of California.

Focus your visit on the lake. The 3.1-mile trail around Lake Merritt can be walked, jogged, or peddled; you can also paddle across it, or ride one of the authentic Venetian gondolas.

pasta with beef shank, flat iron, pork loin, sausage, escarole, spinach, parmigiano, beef reduction).

- **Ramen Shop:** Started by three Chez Panisse alumni, this is one-of-a-kind ramen made with organic and sustainable produce. Come for the noodles, but don't miss the squid and pork fried rice.

- **Joodooboo:** A shop for freshly made tofu and seasonal vegetable preparations that are inspired by Korean flavors and ingredients.

- **Daytrip:** This bustling spot is all about pairing pickled and aged ingredients and naturally fermented wine.

- **Tacos Oscar:** This tiny taqueria in Temescal has outstanding vegetarian items, such as a Charred Brócoli Taco (charred broccoli, peanut-arbol salsa, pickled onion, cilantro).

- **FOB Kitchen:** From-scratch Filipino food paired with excellent cocktails. The crispy chicken skins are hard to resist.

- **Snail Bar:** A natural wine bar and bottle shop with a small, seasonally focused food menu that changes from week to week; Slug Bar is its sister spot.

- **Boichik Bagels:** So good they were featured in the *New York Times*. Don't miss the onion bialy.

BERKELEY

Much like Oakland, Berkeley outings could fill an entire book. Perhaps best known as the home of the University of California, Berkeley—better known as Cal—Berkeley is a college town with a thriving performing arts scene, great restaurants, and outdoor activities. Rather than trying to fit an entire city into two pages, consider this a sampler.

Outdoors:

- **UC Botanical Garden:** Established in 1890 in the hills above campus, these 34 acres make up one of the most diverse landscapes in the world, with over 10,000 types of plants, including many rare and endangered species. Organized geographically, the Garden features nine regions of plantings from Australasia to South Africa, along with a major collection of California native plants. The redwood grove across the street can feel like a mini Muir Woods getaway.

- **Tilden Park:** One of the Park District's three oldest parks, Tilden has been called the jewel of the system, and its recreational activities have become a happy tradition for generations. The park is reached via Canon Drive, Shasta Road, or South Park Drive, all off Grizzly Peak Boulevard in Berkeley. Highlights include:

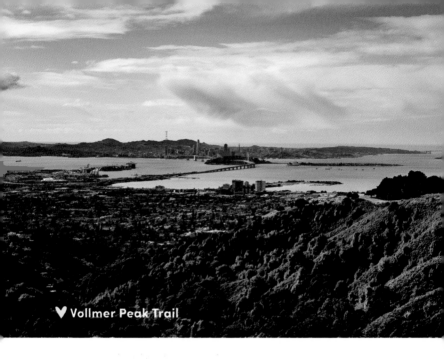

♥ Vollmer Peak Trail

- **The Regional Parks Botanic Garden:** Check out the world's most complete collection of California native plants.

- **Hiking and biking:** There are almost 40 miles of trails in Tilden Park, through many different kinds of terrain. The larger multi use trails allow hikers, bicyclers, and horses; some are for hikers and horses only; and the smaller single-track trails are for hikers only.

- **Lake Anza:** Just over the hill from Berkeley, Tilden Park's Lake Anza is a favorite getaway. Its sandy beach is open to the sun and sheltered from the wind, with lifeguards posted during the swim season.

- **Redwood Valley Railway (Tilden Steam Train):**
  Expect a lot of kids, but this scaled-down steam
  train offers rides along a scenic ridge.

Campus Wanders:

- **Berkeley Landmarks Tour:** Cal is famous for the
  number of structures it has listed in the National
  Register of Historic Places.

- **Hayward Fault Tour:** Learn about the earthquake
  fault that runs through campus.

- **Campus Public Art + Architecture:** This map
  offers three self-guided tours, each featuring UC
  Berkeley's most significant works of public art and
  a varying range of architectural styles that span
  nearly 150 years.

- **Walking Tour of the Berkeley Bears:** The Berkeley
  Library created a campus map with locations and
  descriptions of 23 bear statues and artwork found
  throughout the university's grounds.

- **Eucalyptus Grove:** In 1882, a grove of Tasmanian
  blue gums (Eucalyptus globulus) was planted as a
  windbreak for the old cinder running track. It is the
  tallest stand of hardwood trees in North America
  and the tallest stand of this type of eucalyptus in
  the world.

- **Indian Rock Park:** Located in northeast Berkeley, this park provides great views and picnic spots along with and challenges for early-level rock climbing.

The Arts

- **Greek Theater:** The William Randolph Hearst Greek Theatre is located on the UC Berkeley Campus in the foothills, with spectacular views of San Francisco's skyline. It is the longest-running outdoor amphitheater in the country—opened on September 24, 1903—and continues to be one of the top area venues. You can sit on the amphitheater seats or on the grass above. Either way, a picnic and a blanket are highly recommended.

- **Berkeley Art Museum:** The Berkeley Art Museum and Pacific Film Archive are a combined art museum, repertory movie theater, and archive. The museum's holdings include an emphasis on twentieth- and twenty-first-century work, including abstract expressionist painting, contemporary photography, conceptual art, and African American quilts, along with focused historical collections of nineteenth-century American folk art and early American painting, Italian Baroque painting, Old Master works on paper, and East Asian paintings. The film archive includes more than 18,000 films and videos, representing the largest collection of Japanese cinema outside of Japan and impressive

♥ Sather Tower

holdings of Soviet cinema, West Coast avant-garde film, and seminal video art, as well as hundreds of thousands of articles, reviews, posters, and other ephemera related to the history of film.

- **Berkeley Rep:** Known for its core values of imagination and excellence, as well as its educated and adventurous audience, Berkeley Rep has been a welcoming home for emerging and established artists since 1968.

- **Freight & Salvage Coffeehouse:** The longest-running full-time folk and traditional music venue west of the Mississippi puts on shows in a 440-seat, green-and-LEED-certified venue downtown.

- **Cal Performances:** Cal Performances presents over 100 events annually in five venues—Zellerbach Hall, Zellerbach Playhouse, Hertz Hall, and Wheeler Hall on the UC Berkeley campus, and First Congregational Church of Berkeley. The performances range among dance, theater, chamber music, jazz, and world music.

Eat & Drink

Berkeley is the birthplace of California Cuisine, and today those core values of menus built around local and seasonal products are found in myriad eclectic restaurants.

- **Chez Panisse:** Open for more than 50 years, Chez

Panisse is legendary. There is a downstairs option with set menus that do not fit within the budget category, as well as an upstairs cafe where you can split a salad, pizza, and dessert and enjoy a more casual version of what's offered downstairs.

- **The Cheeseboard Collective:** Whether you are looking for cheese, bread and pastries for a picnic, or some of the best pizza around, the Cheese Board should be on your Berkeley list. The cheese shop-bakery is open Wednesday through Saturday. The Pizzeria serves hot pizza and salad Thursday through Saturday in the evening.

- **Lulu:** An ode to the chef's childhood with a modern, fresh, and timeless California take on Palestinian cuisine. The menu is anchored in a robust bread program, pastries with spins on traditional flavors, seasonal salads and sandwiches available daily, and a mezze brunch on the weekends.

- **Fish & Bird Sousaku Izakaya:** Contemporary Japanese cuisine from a chef classically trained in Japanese and French cooking techniques. They source local, seasonal, and sustainable ingredients, augmented with specialty items imported from Japan, and offer a highly curated selection of local and Japanese sake, beer, shochu, wine, and spirits.

OCEAN BEACH

San Francisco has many beaches, including Baker Beach, with its beautiful views, and the beach at Ft. Funston, where dogs and their humans can enjoy an off-leash frolic. But Ocean Beach's 3.5-mile-wide stretch of sand has the most options for a choose-your-own-adventure sort of date any time of day, as well as the most spots to simply settle down on a blanket to watch the waves, sunset, or surfers. Of note for those not familiar with the area, pay attention to the signs highlighting the rip currents that make swimming a very bad idea. Dip your toes, but take care. Also know that Ocean Beach is often foggy, which is a great excuse to cuddle under a warm blanket.

Other recommended options include taking advantage of the breeze to fly a kite (a good chance to see how well you work together), searching for sea glass and sand dollars near the tide line (free mementos!), and people watching as you stroll, hand

ABOUT THOSE BONFIRES

There are 16 available fire rings and the National Park Service does not require permits for groups of fewer than 25 people. The rings tend to go quickly on weekends, but if you are willing to get there early or to come on a weekday, a fire is quite possible. And what's more romantic than watching a sunset fireside cuddled up with someone special?

in hand, either along the beach or above along the Great Highway. Plus, the beach has an amazing sunset, including a reflection on the water that makes for a great photo, and the opportunity for bonfires at night.

▼ For Your Picnic

As befits a beach with day and night options, nearby takeout spots have options from breakfast through dinner.

- **Devil's Teeth Bakery:** Get the breakfast sandwiches and cinnamon rolls.

- **AndyTown:** Take care of your need for caffeine and pastries that will warm you on a windy beach day.

- **Plam City Wine:** The hoagies are a strong contender for the best sandwich in San Francisco. Plus, their wine-and-beer selection is delightful.

- **Hook Fish Company:** Impeccably fresh fish for sale and prepared items such as poke, fish tacos, and fish-and-chips.

ANGEL ISLAND

Alcatraz gets a lot of deserved attention, but lesser-known Angel Island has some of the best views of the city and surrounding area. On a clear day, Sonoma

GET OUT OF TOWN   141

♥ **Summit of Angel Island**

and Napa can be seen from the north side of the island and San Jose can be seen from the south side. Access to the island is by private boat or public ferry, the Blue and Gold from San Francisco and the Angel Island Ferry from Tiburon. Once on the island, you can hike, bike, take a tram tour, or simply picnic or dine with a view.

There are two restaurants on the island: the Cafe and the Cantina. You can also order ahead and pick up a boxed lunch from Angel Island Café or bring supplies with you.

♥ **Recommended hikes include:**

- **Perimeter Trail:** The perimeter trail offers views of the entire San Francisco Bay along the 5.5-mile loop around the island. This is the most popular trail on the island and is open to hikers and bikes (rentals available at the island on a first come basis). The route offers a variety of views; on a clear day from the San Francisco side of the island near Battery Ledyard, one can see the Golden Gate Bridge, Bay Bridge, and Alcatraz from a single vantage point.

- **Mt. Livermore:** The peak of Mt. Livermore is 788 feet tall and has views that span all of the island and Bay Area from its top. There are two routes: one following the Sunset Trail and one following the North Ridge Trail. The summit is a perfect place for a picnic.

- **Immigration Station Trail:** The hike includes 144 trail stairs beginning and ending in Ayala Cove. You can tour the grounds and outdoor interpretive displays, as well as visit the USIS museum to see the restored detention areas and Chinese poetry engraved on the walls. Distance is approximately 2 miles round trip.

"THE ELLIS ISLAND OF THE WEST"

More than 300,000 people from 80 countries passed through the small immigration station off the San Francisco coast before entering the US during the early 1900s You can walk there or take a tram ride.

ALCATRAZ NIGHT TOUR

A prison visit as a date? Indeed, if it is an evening visit to Alcatraz. You can enjoy a sunset ferry ride and hear compelling stories about the island's history and residents. The Alcatraz Night Tour is limited to just a few hundred visitors per evening and includes special programs, tours, and activities not offered during the day. If the timing works for you, a night with a full or near full-moon will provide breathtaking photos of moonrise over the Bay Bridge. parksconservancy.org/services/alcatraz-tours

For a pre- or post-visit meal beyond the bacon-wrapped hotdogs available outside the gate, there are some options below. If you are coming or going from downtown, the Ferry Building is a convenient stop; see page 86.

- **Buena Vista Cafe:** Is it a mile walk? Yes? But will you want an Irish coffee after your trip to the rock? Also, yes.

- **Scoma's:** Also about a mile away, this classic seafood spot is many locals' answer when asked: Where should I eat near the wharf? Impeccable seafood, a waterfront view, and classic cocktails make this a perfect spot to complete your evening.

- **Fog Harbor Fish House:** Situated in a prime-time spot on Pier 39 in Fisherman's Wharf, Fog Harbor offers a big outdoor space with views of the bay and bridge.

♥ **Alcatraz Island**

- **La Mar:** Head back toward downtown along the Embarcadero for this modern Peruvian restaurant that boasts tall ceilings and big views of the bay.

- **Abaca:** If you are heading toward Fisherman's Wharf, Abaca features contemporary Filipino Californian fare, like pork skewers with banana BBQ sauce, salmon kinilaw, and chorizo-stuffed squid.

LET'S MEET FOR A DRINK

Is there a more classic date than coffee or perhaps a cocktail? Probably not. This section looks at options for both, but also highlights classic bars, rooftop options, and more. Much like in the restaurant section, Shared Spaces has greatly increased outdoor options and you will see that reflected here.

ROOFTOP BARS

Perhaps due to local legend Karl the Fog (yes, the fog has an unofficial official name), for many years San Francisco was lacking in rooftop bars, with a few notable exceptions. In recent years there has been a boom, however. Most have heaters, but an extra sweater, sweatshirt, or a blanket to cuddle under is never a bad idea.

- **Charmaine's:** On top of the Proper Hotel on Market Street, Charmaine's features gorgeous views (City Hall at sunset is a highlight), fire pits, and cocktails from the team behind Bon Vivants and Trick Dog. Snacks and full meals are available.

- **El Techo:** El Techo has long been one of the city's best options for outdoor drinking, day or night. Head up to the rooftop patio overlooking Mission Street for margaritas, small plates, and both brunch and happy hour.

- **Rooftop 25:** Rooftop 25 at 25 Lusk in SoMa is spacious, with glass windscreens as well as heaters and string lights. Food highlights include wood-fired pizzas and caviar and blinis, if you are feeling fancy.

- **Kaiyō Rooftop:** Perched high above the SoMa skyline atop the Hyatt Place hotel, this offshoot of

the Cow Hollow favorite offers a menu of Peruvian Nikkei food and drinks including sushi rolls, ceviches, and tropical-inspired cocktails.

- **Fiorella Sunset/Bar Nonnina:** A somewhat secret rooftop deck in the inner Sunset where you can enjoy pizzas and negronis under the string lights.

- **Good Good Culture Club:** From the team behind Liholiho Yacht Club, a massive, colorful and plant-filled rooftop deck with a menu of food and drink inspired by cuisines across the Asian diaspora.

- **Jones:** One of the city's biggest rooftop spaces, but keep in mind that even though the outdoor area is technically on a rooftop, it's more of a patio one-story above street level in the Tenderloin, so you won't be getting sweeping views. On the other hand, you may very well get a table.

- **Dirty Habit:** On the fifth floor of the Hotel Zeto, this spot feels secluded and you can choose from a table for a full meal or a couch for more of a lounge feel.

INDOOR VIEWS

- **Cityscape Lounge:** At 46 stories, Cityscape in the Hilton is the tallest sky bar in San Francisco with 360° views that may be the very best in town.

- **Top of the Mark:** A fixture for eight decades, the Top of the Mark offers spectacular views of the San Francisco skyline from the hotel's nineteenth floor. The historic lounge serves up creative cocktails and signature martinis.

DRINK OUTSIDE

There is something about drinking outside that makes people happy. The following spots offer excellent drinks, most have food options, and all are welcoming both on sunny days and foggy nights.

- **Horsefeather:** This bar on Divisadero Street has excellent cocktails and food, plus a fully covered outdoor, street-side seating area. Note that they serve brunch on the weekends until 4pm.

- **The Page:** The Divisadero spot has stiff cocktails, plenty of beers on tap (23 to be exact), and a casual atmosphere.

- **Zeitgeist:** The iconic Mission bar and beer garden has long been a destination for sunny days and bundled-up nights.

- **Wild Side West:** The Bernal Heights lesbian bar's lush outdoor garden has been drawing in people with reasonably priced drinks since 1976.

- **Casements:** This Irish bar has live music and other special events, a huge outdoor patio, and some of the best fish-and-chips around.

- **Anina:** This Hayes Valley spot features a sun-drenched patio with twinkle lights and plenty of outdoor picnic tables.

- **Red Window:** With sangria and more, this North Beach spot has two covered and heated parklets.

- **Biergarten:** This Hayes Valley parking lot beer garden has excellent German beer, pretzels, and bratwurst.

- **Lost Resort:** This nautical-themed Mission bar has a large back patio and a full food menu both at dinner and brunch.

- **Ungrafted:** This Dogpatch wine shop has a super wine list, plenty of parklet seating, and an appealing menu of things like charcuterie and cheese plates, salt and vinegar fries, pastas, and sandwiches.

- **El Rio:** This Bernal Heights bar describes itself as your friendly queer neighborhood bar, community space, and patio. Recognized as a Legacy Business by the San Francisco Small Business Commission, it is best known for supporting the community by providing a space for gatherings, LGBTQ+ performances, music and dancing, and community fundraising events.

- **20 Spot:** Local brews, wine, and modern American fare from snacks to full meals, with heaters for outdoor dining and drinking in this cozy . . . spot.

CLASSIC BARS

San Francisco is full of new and innovative bars, with more opening regularly. Places like Eater and Thrillist run regular "Hottest Bars" lists and those are great resources when looking at the coolest and most of-the-moment places. The bars below, instead, represent some of San Francisco's best classic bars, places that have withstood the pressures of time and the ever-changing city real estate market to be, as the dictionary says, of lasting worth.

- **Old Ship Saloon:** This Jackson Square bar was built upon the ruins of a Gold Rush–era ship that ran aground in 1849. The ship was hauled to the then-shore in the Barbary Coast area of the city. Eventually it was covered with landfill, and the building that now houses Old Ship was constructed above it. To drink? The Gold Rush, with bourbon, lemon, and honey.

- **Elixir:** This is the second-oldest continually operating saloon location in San Francisco, making it one of the most historic bars in the country. They have documented evidence of saloon service on this corner since at least 1858. To drink? A Scofflaw: bourbon, Martini & Rossi Dry, lemon, grenadine, bitters.

- **Shotwell's:** First opened over 100 years ago, the corner of 20th Street and Shotwell originally started as a Grocery Saloon. After The Great Quake of 1906, the owner scrapped the grocery half and dedicated the space entirely to a saloon. To drink? Beer, wine, or cider; no cocktails available.

- **Homestead:** Established in 1902, the Homestead has been a brothel and a speakeasy. Settle in at a spot near the wood-burning stove and dig into a basket of peanuts. To drink? Your favorite.

- **Hotel Utah:** Built in 1908, The Hotel Utah Saloon remains a SoMa neighborhood hangout for drinks, live music, and food. To drink? A local beer.

- **House of Shields:** Open since 1908, House of Shields is a historic San Francisco landmark. To honor tradition, it doesn't have a clock or TV on the premises. Trivia: The House of Shields was also a favorite spot of President Warren G. Harding. To drink? A Martinez.

- **Vesuvio:** Established in 1948, this bar was a hang-out for Beat Generation celebrities including Jack Kerouac, Allen Ginsberg, Lawrence Ferlinghetti, and Neal Cassady and remains a living monument to jazz, poetry, and art. To drink? A Jack Kerouac with rum, tequila, fruit juice, and lime.

- **Tommy's Mexican:** Family run for more than 50 years, with more than 300 tequilas to choose from, Tommy's has one of the best selections on the planet. To drink? The agave-syrup-enhanced margarita, a recipe that remains unchanged since 1965.

- **Twin Peaks Tavern:** Designated a historical bar in 2013, this is the first known gay bar to feature full-length open plate-glass windows, openly revealing the identities of their patrons. Sitting at the intersection of Castro and Market Streets, Twin Peaks stands as a gateway into the neighborhood. To drink? One of their hot coffee-options.

- **Philosopher's Club:** Located in West Portal, this bar is famous as the home of the man who started mixology, Jerry Thomas (he wrote the first book on the topic). Come for the history and the quotes on the ceiling, but stay for the drinks. To drink? Your regular.

- **Zam Zam:** Legendary San Francisco columnist Herb Caen once described Zam Zam as "a place that time forgot, its curving bar filled with worshipers sitting in silent contemplation of the silver bullet in its graceful stemmed glass." To drink? A martini.

- **Comstock Saloon:** Restored to its original glory in 2010, the Comstock Saloon occupies a historic space at the crossroads of North Beach, Chinatown, Financial District, and Jackson Square. To drink? Pisco Punch with pisco, pineapple gum, lemon, and secrets.

- **Specs:** Once described by the *San Francisco Chronicle* as "a home to a menagerie of misfits, from strippers and poets to longshoremen and merchant marines," the bar is officially named Specs' Twelve Adler Museum Cafe. To drink? An Anchor Steam.

- **Tony Nik's:** Tony Nik's was originally home to Madame Nicco's French Laundry, owned and operated by Angelina and Antonio 'Tony' Nicco during the 1920s Prohibition era and the 1930s Depression years. When Prohibition was repealed in 1933, Tony immediately opened Tony Nicco's Café, one of the first bars to open in North Beach. Tony Nicco's was called a cafe because, at that time, food was required to be served with alcohol. To drink? A manhattan.

- **Redwood Room:** On December 5, 1933, the 21st Amendment was adopted, repealing the 18th Amendment, which had outlawed the sale, transport, and manufacture of "intoxicating liquors." The very next day, on December 6, 1933, The Clift's iconic Redwood Room opened to great acclaim. The now legal speakeasy was an immediate hit with everyone from local residents to national celebrities, due to the moody atmosphere, creative cocktails, dramatic redwood paneling, and eclectic mix of patrons. To drink? A Rob Roy.

- **Dogpatch Saloon:** Dating back to 1912, this bar is even dog-friendly. To drink? A Greyhound or a Salty Dog.

- **The Saloon:** This bar has been in continuous operation since opening in 1861. To drink? Whiskey, straight.

- **Pied Piper:** A classic bar in a classic hotel. Since 1909, Maxfield Parrish's famed Pied Piper painting has hung at the bar of the same name inside of the legendary Palace Hotel. To drink? The Charlie Chaplin with rye, absinthe, Dubonnet, and bitters.

BEER

Does your date's online profile talk about a love of sours? Does a flight of beers sound better to you than a flight of wine? A beer-focused date may be for you. San Francisco is a city with both locally made brews and bars with a large selection of some of the finest imported and domestic collections around.

- **Toronado:** This lower Haight spot is an institution that features over 40 beers on tap.

- **Monks Kettle:** Upscale pub food and a broad and balanced craft beer list, including a large selection of Belgian and Trappist beers.

- **City Beer Store:** An extremely large number of beers to buy, but also a large patio for in-person sipping.

- **Cellarmaker:** You can and should visit their SoMa location, but don't miss the Bernal location for some of SF's best Detroit-style pizza with your beer.

- **Anchor:** Now owned by Sapporo, the brewery offers public tours and tastings, but if you can, also head to Public Taps (an indoor/outdoor space across the street from the brewery), where you'll find beers exclusively brewed for the space.

- **21st Amendment:** Located very close to Oracle Park and named after the amendment that ended

Prohibition, it is particularly known for its seasonal beers, specifically Hell or High Watermelon wheat beer.

- **Barebottle:** This Bernal warehouse-style space with ample seating features beers brewed on-site, plus a rotating schedule of visiting food trucks.

- **Barrel Head Brewhouse:** If you are looking for something for everyone, Barrel Head is a great choice as it features house-made beers, guest brews, cocktails, and a full food menu.

- **Fort Point:** With a main brewery at Crissy Field (not open to the public), Fort Point came onto the local beer scene in 2014 and found instant popularity. The

Ferry Building kiosk features rotating beer picks, plus growlers and chilled six-packs to-go.

- **Laughing Monk:** Small-batch, inventive California-meets-Belgian-style beer, but also frequent activities like trivia, pinball, collabs with other breweries, and food trucks. In their words, they are "traditionally irreverent, inspired by the pastimes of Belgium, but always in the spirit of California's innovative mindset."

- **Woods Beer & Beer Co:** With multiple locations in the city, including on Treasure Island, Woods makes creative, small-batch beer and wine inspired by nature, place, and tradition. The tap rooms all have a theme—the Russian Hill spot is modeled on a ski chalet, the Mission one on an Argentine estancia.

- **Speakeasy:** The Prohibition era-themed taproom features the core beers that can be found in store, seasonal brews, one-offs from Hunters Point Brewery, and guest taps from breweries.

- **Park Chalet:** Located in a historic building at the edge of Golden Gate Park, just across the street from Ocean Beach, this is a beer garden with stellar views of the Pacific and a solid selection of food and drink.

- **Black Hammer:** This SoMa brewery focuses on balanced lagers, ales, and hard seltzers.

- **New Belgium:** Located in Mission Bay, close to both the Giants and the Warriors, you can order a bunch of the New Belgium classics, but what you should do instead is try the small-batch releases brewed on-site.

COFFEE

Is there a more classic first date than coffee? A necessity for some, a pleasure for others, coffee houses are also a great place to become regulars or grab a morning or midday pick-me-up for your sweetie. It is also a great way to explore the different neighborhoods across the city.

- **Grand Coffee:** With two locations on Mission Street, Grand calls itself the "stoop of the neighborhood." Along with coffee, they have non-coffee drinks including a Lime Rickey and pastries from local bakeries.

- **Linea Cafe:** With two cafes, one in the Mission District and another in Potrero Hill, Linea has won awards from the likes of the Good Food Foundation for their roasts.

- **Saint Frank:** Saint Frank is known for its pour-over coffees and espresso drinks, made with beans from independent producers. Don't miss the house Almond Macadamia Milk.

- **Equator:** This LGBTQ+-founded, BCorp-certified roaster has many locations across the area, including at the Round House at the Golden Gate Bridge, a 1937 Art Deco building with amazing views of Golden Gate National Recreation Area.

- **Red Bay:** Founded in 2014 by Keba Konte, Red Bay Coffee, is, in their words: "at the forefront of what we believe is the fourth wave of coffee—a firm commitment to ensure coffee production is not only high quality and sustainable, but a vehicle for diversity, inclusion, social and economic restoration, entrepreneurship, and environmental sustainability."

- **Fluid Cooperative:** Located inside La Cocina's Municipal Marketplace in the Tenderloin, the cafe is run by three trans leaders, activists, and artists striving to create an inclusive, welcoming, and nurturing space for trans, non-binary, and gender-non-conforming youth and community members.

- **Hey Neighbor:** This black- and queer-owned shop has a lot of things going for it, including the fact that they have a cafe cat. They host many special events, so be sure to check out their socials.

- **Andytown:** Founded in 2014 to bring specialty coffee roasting to the Outer Sunset, there are now three locations there and one location downtown. For those looking for something out of the ordinary, try the Snowy Plover with sparkling water over ice, espresso, brown sugar syrup, and whipped cream.

- **Farley's:** Established in 1989, this is a Potrero Hill mainstay—a real community hub that also hosts events like an annual Halloween pet parade and costume contest.

- **Flywheel:** Located in the Haight near Golden Gate Park, Flywheel has both a full cafe with indoor and outdoor seating and a kiosk across the street.

- **Rise & Grind:** With locations on 8th Avenue near Golden Gate Park and in the Mission, Rise & Grind features all the classics, but also specialty options like a Chagaccino, a mushroom latte booster— made with cacao, cinnamon, and sweetened with monk fruit and mixed with double espresso and steamed milk.

- **Sextant:** This SoMa roaster was founded by Kinani Ahmed, a first-generation Ethiopian who works directly with farmers across Ethiopia, Kenya, Colombia, and elsewhere in order to showcase the most flavorful coffees throughout the world.

- **Haus:** The 24th Street shop has a great backyard patio.

- **Coffee Movement:** This Nob Hill spot serves coffee daily from 7:00am until 4:00pm. Don't miss their signature, Tasting Flight: three pours of the day's featured coffees, or one coffee prepared three different ways.

- **Sightglass:** With locations in SoMa, the Mission, and on Divisadero Street, this sibling-owned roast-ery takes its name from the "sightglass," the viewing window on their vintage PROBAT coffee roaster that exposes the complex and delicate process of roasting coffee.

- **Wrecking Ball:** Founded in 2011, Wrecking Ball's Union Street location serves a full menu of espresso drinks, brewed coffee, hand crafted pour-over coffee on a custom-built brew bar, as well as a selection of teas and herbal tisanes.

- **Graffeo Coffee:** Founded in 1935 in North Beach, this is one of North America's oldest artisan coffee roasters and remains a family-run company passed on down through generations.

- **California Khave:** This latest location of this charming coffee caravan can be found on social media; along with coffee, be sure to grab Dynamo donuts and New Zealand baked goods.

- **DamnFine:** This favorite pizza spot now has a cafe featuring excellent coffee, plus house-made focaccia toasts.

- **Excelsior Coffee:** Calling itself a hardworking coffee joint in love with its neighborhood, "inspired to bring dope coffee to dope folks," it hosts frequent pop-up events.

LIVE

San Franciscans are lucky to live in a place that is not only the home of highly talented local performers, but is also a stop for most national tours. Which means that whether you like jazz, classical, or musical theater, there is a venue for you. This section also includes spectator sports, music festivals, and games and activities including roller skating and bowling.

CHURCH OF 8 WHEELS

Is it time for a couple's skate? Those with memories—or just movie memories—of childhood roller rinks will be delighted to visit San Francisco's only indoor rink. In true San Francisco fashion, rather than a 1970s-style rink, the Church of 8 Wheels is, as the name suggests, located in a decommissioned church on Fillmore Street. Rest assured, though, there are still lessons, skate rental, and the opportunity to book a flashback date.

Looking to extend your date? It is about a 10-minute walk to Divisadero Street favorites, like one of the best burgers in town at Nopa, Horsefeather's delightful cocktails, and more. Hayes Valley is also a 10-minute walk and spots such as Salt & Straw (try the ice cream flight!) and the popular Souvla (don't miss the Greek fries) are a great way to continue a casual night. Even closer are the Lower Haight bars and restaurants including beer bar Toronado and Otra's modern Mexican cuisine.

Fallen in love with roller skating? You'll need to bring your own skates, but there are regular community skate events at the SkatePark (Skatin' Place) located near 6th Avenue in Golden Gate Park. Best known of these events is their Sunday roller disco party. As of summer 2022, the area features a large-scale mural, "Psychedelic Golden Gate Skate," that pays homage to the area's decades-long history as a meeting space for skaters.

Rather dance without skates? Try Lindy in the Park, each Sunday behind the De Young Museum. Fun to watch or participate in, it features free social swing dancing every Sunday (weather permitting, of course) from 11:00am–2:00pm. There are free beginners lessons most Sundays from 12–12:30.

LIVE MUSIC

Whether it is going to see the band who sings "your song" or introducing your date to a favorite band new to them, San Francisco has many venues for live music. From stadium-esque venues like The Bill Graham Civic Auditorium to small clubs and bars with a band a night or two a week, there is live music available in most neighborhoods and most nights. And seasonal programs and festivals—like Hardly Strictly Bluegrass and the concerts at Stern Grove—provide even more opportunities to see all sorts of acts in amazing outdoor settings (see page 176).

- **SFJAZZ Center:** Located in Hayes Valley, near many great food and drink options, the SFJAZZ Center includes the 700-seat Robert N. Miner Auditorium and the 100-seat Joe Henderson Lab. What that means for you is a first-class spot with shows year-round, featuring both big names and up-and-coming artists.

♥ Hardly Strictly Bluegrass

- **Boom Boom Room:** Calling itself San Francisco's funkiest club, this is a great spot for live music most nights, and a great place to go before a show at the Fillmore.

- **The Fillmore:** Looking to take in some history with your music? Opened in 1912 and operating as the Fillmore Auditorium since 1954, this has been a must-do for generations of San Francisco music fans. Don't miss the posters that highlight some of the venue's historic shows, and don't forget to take home a poster at the end of the night. Of note: there are very few seats at the Fillmore, so expect to stand and likely dance.

- **Bottom of the Hill:** Once named the Best Place to See Live Music in San Francisco by *Rolling Stone*, this Portero Hill spot presents a wide range of artists nightly. It also features a full bar, kitchen, and outdoor patio.

- **The Independent:** The Independent is frequently called no-frills, but that doesn't mean it isn't a great place to see a show. Plus nearby hotspots on Divisadero Street can provide excellent drinks and food.

- **Great American Music Hall:** Located in the Tenderloin, its decorative balconies, columns, and frescoes make for an amazing atmosphere.

- **Bimbo's 365 Club:** A San Francisco landmark located in North Beach, Bimbo's 365 features art deco detailing, a dance floor, but also comfortable seating, a plus for a more intimate date.

- **The Warfield:** The Warfield is a 2,250-person venue originally opened on May 13, 1922. Of note: there is generally both a standing-room-only section on the main floor and extensive reserved seating available.

SPECTATOR SPORTS

In 2022 the Golden State Warriors, now playing in San Francisco, won their fourth NBA title in eight years. The San Francisco Giants won the World Series in 2010, 2012, and 2014. Across the bay, the Oakland A's have won nine World Series championships and 15 AL pennants. The 49ers, who have decamped from San Francisco and actually play 38 miles south of the city in Santa Clara, have long been considered one of the most storied franchises in the NFL.

All of this is to say: Bay Area sports fans are used to success. A negative of all of that success? A's excepted, tickets tend to be expensive. That said, the stadiums are, in general, a joy to visit and reflect the teams' achievements.

- **Chase Center:** Although some may miss the Warriors' former Oakland home, it would be hard to not enjoy a game here, even if you are a casual fan. The food is a highlight, the arena is state of the art, and the location in Mission Bay means that there are plenty of spots to enjoy drinks pre- or post-game.

- **Oracle Park:** The home of the Giants since 2000 and a delight both for serious fans and casual viewers. The location is excellent, walkable from downtown and situated along San Francisco Bay.

Indeed, the section of the bay beyond Oracle Park's right field wall is unofficially known as McCovey Cove, in honor of former Giants player Willie McCovey and a popular spot for pleasure boats and kayakers. The Portwalk, located beyond the outfield wall, allows you to take in sweeping views of the bay while strolling along the water's edge. You can also view the game, free of charge, for up to three innings or longer, depending on the size of the crowd.

- **Levi's Stadium:** The most important thing to know about this Santa Clara arena is that it is far enough from the city that locals often laugh when broadcasters show images of the Golden Gate Bridge on telecasts. That said, it has been praised for its excellent sightlines, beautiful architecture, plentiful amenities, technological advancements, and—like Chase Center and Oracle Park—its great food. Of note: due to its location, it is frequently much warmer and sunnier than in San Francisco, so be prepared.

The Bay Area is also home to the San Jose Sharks for NHL hockey, the San Jose Earthquake of Major League Soccer, the Oakland Roots of the USL Championship soccer league, and several minor-league teams.

Looking for something a little lower key? The University of San Francisco men's basketball team, once a powerhouse, made its first NCAA tournament in twenty-plus years in 2022.

Cal boasts numerous highly successful teams. Stanford, located in Palo Alto on the Peninsula, is one of the most dominant sports schools in the country. Of particular note is their women's basketball team, a perennial title favorite and a remarkably affordable team to watch play.

PLAY A GAME

Interested in a little friendly competition? You can show off your skills (or lack thereof) at several bowling alleys or miniature golf courses around town. Plus, in true San Francisco fashion, many of them feature adult drinks to help set the mood and salve the agony of gutter balls and missed putts.

- **Presidio Bowl:** Built when the Presidio was still a military base, Presidio Bowl features 12 lanes, over 45 beers, 19 wines by the glass, and a very popular burger. Friday and Saturday nights feature glow-in-the-dark bowling!

- **Yerba Buena Ice Skating and Bowling Center:** This 12-lane bowling alley may have few thrills, but it does offer you the chance for a couple's skate after your game. Plus, the downtown location makes it an easy pre-cocktail stop.

- **Mission Bowling Club:** Cocktails more your style? Looking to combine your bowling with one of the best burgers in town? This is your place. Note that there are only 6 lanes, so reservations are suggested.

- **Urban Putt:** Located in the Mission, this is an indoor, 14-hole miniature golf course. The golf is first come, first served, but you can reserve at the on-site restaurant for dinner after your round. Expect golf puns on the menu.

- **Subpar Miniature Golf:** Take an 18-hole tour around the city at this Ghirardelli Square spot.

There are on-site drinks and snacks available, but for a sweet end to your date, don't miss the classic and neighborhood favorite Ghirardelli hot fudge sundae.

- **Stagecoach Greens:** The city's only outdoor mini golf course! Take a tour of San Francisco on this course, designed to tell a story of boom and bust in the West and explore the elements that shaped the city. Plus, the course is adjacent to ParkLab Gardens, featuring daily food trucks and an on-site bar. Note that tee time reservations are required.

- **Thriller Social Club:** A bar with a Skee-Ball arena with 8 classic lanes, a boxing test of strength, a golf simulator, a baseball pitching game, Pop-A-Shot basketball, and much more.

FESTIVALS

All the world's a stage. Or perhaps in San Francisco every park is a stage? The city's temperate climate makes it possible to host outdoor events in parks and venues throughout the year.

- **Stern Grove Festival:** Celebrating its 85th season in 2022, Stern Grove is a natural amphitheater surrounded by giant eucalyptus, redwood, and fir trees; it is one of Northern California's favorite

Stern Grove Festival

concert sites, presenting—for free!—award winners, legends, and exciting new artists to thousands of attendees each year. There are food trucks on-site, but this is a great opportunity to show your picnic creativity! Note: concerts have always been free and open to the public, but in 2022, reservations were required. Keep an eye on their website for future plans.

- **Hardly Strictly Bluegrass:** An annual free-to-the-public festival, Hardly Strictly Bluegrass takes place in the heart of Golden Gate Park during the first weekend in October. An eclectic lineup of country, soul, folk, and more performs nonstop across multiple outdoor stages. You can bring a picnic, but there are food vendors on-site.

- **Outside Lands:** Outside Lands is a three-day festival celebrating music, food, wine, beer, and art. It features big-name headline bands, elaborate food and drink offerings, and much more. It is also very much not free and is open to the public, with tickets often selling out in advance.

- **San Francisco Mime Troupe:** These may not be the mimes you are thinking of. Rather than a silent performance, expect political satire in story and song. Every summer, they perform in San Francisco Bay Area parks, July 4 through Labor Day. After the performance the actors and musicians come out into the audience to pass the hat.

- **SF Shakespeare Festival:** Shakespeare in the park staged every year in San Francisco and beyond from July to October, providing an opportunity to see high-quality, professional theater free of charge.

Indoor:

- **Noise Pop:** An annual week-long music and arts festival that takes place throughout the San Francisco Bay Area.

- **SF Jazz Festival:** SF Jazz is a joy year-round, but their annual festival presents an opportunity to see an all-star lineup over a week-plus of shows. Performances take place at both the SFJAZZ Center and additional select venues.

ARTY OUTINGS

World-class museums, public art, bookstores, and films are just a few of the things you'll find in this section.

MISSION MURAL MEANDER

San Francisco is a city with many murals, but the Mission is known for having the highest concentration, with murals dating from the 1970s to the present. You can find them on businesses, churches, private homes, and in alleys that are more often seen just as shortcuts to BART.

While you can easily spend an afternoon discovering delights without a map, beginning at either the 16th or 24th Street BART stations, a great place to start a more organized tour is at Precita Eyes Mural Arts and Visitor Center, where you can buy a Mission District Mural Map; they also offer guided mural tours.

A SWEET TREAT FOR YOUR WALK

The Mission has some of the city's best ice cream shops, including Humphry Slocombe, Garden Creamery, Nieves Cinco de Mayo, and Bi-Rite Creamery.

And see page 66 for taco crawl suggestions.

♥ **Three murals not to miss are:**

- **Balmy Alley between 24th and 25th Streets, and Treat and Harrison Streets:** The murals began in the mid-,80s as an expression of artists' outrage over human rights and political abuses in Central America. Today the alley contains murals of varied styles and subjects, from human rights to local gentrification.

- **Clarion Alley between 17th and 18th Streets, and Mission and Valencia Streets:** The mission of Clarion Alley Mural Project (CAMP) is to support and produce socially engaged and aesthetically innovative public art, locally and globally, as a grassroots, artist-run organization based in San Francisco's Mission District. There have been over 900 murals created since 1992.

- **MaestraPeace on the Women's Building at 3543 18th Street between Valencia and Guerrero:** MaestraPeace Mural was painted in 1994 by a Who's Who of Bay Area muralists: Juana Alicia, Miranda Bergman, Edythe Boone, Susan Kelk Cervantes, Meera Desai, Yvonne Littleton, and

Irene Perez. One of San Francisco's largest and best-known murals, MaestraPeace serves as a visual testament to the courageous contributions of women through time and around the world.

Looking for more information about some of the murals you see? SFMOMA has created the online Proyecto Mission Murals, which provides information on the artists, titles, and additional details.

FILM FESTIVALS

Film festivals are a monthly, if not weekly, occurrence in San Francisco. Which means that there is something for almost everyone. Serious fans can plan to see as many as possible, while more casual moviegoers can dip in and out. Check out filmsf.org/local-film-festivals.

The SF Film Festival: This is the longest-running film festival in the Americas. Founded in 1957, the annual April event features a range of marquee premieres, international competitions, documentaries, short and mid-length films, and larger events. Movies are shown at theaters across the city including the historic Castro Theater.

- **SF Doc Fest:** As the name suggests, SF Doc Fest is an annual festival devoted to documentary cinema. Since 2001, this event has brought real life to the big screen.

- **Frameline:** Founded in 1977, the San Francisco International LGBTQ+ Film Festival is the longest-running, largest, and most widely recognized LGBTQ+ film exhibition event in the world. It is held in late June to coincide with Pride.

- **Noir City:** A Bay Area celebration of all things noir since 2003. After many years at the Castro Theater, the 2022 edition took place at the Grand Lake Theater in Oakland.

- **Silent Film Festival:** For the last 25 years, a celebration of silent film. Leonard Maltin has called it "a feast for lovers of classic film and live music that is as elaborate, ambitious, and masterfully mounted as any I've seen."

- **International Ocean Film Festival:** IOFF produces a festival of ocean-themed films from all over the world. Themes range from marine science and industry to sports and adventure. The goal is to entertain, educate, and encourage active participation in ocean conservation.

- **Dance Film Festival:** The large range of dance films shown at multiple venues around town highlight everything from "screendance," short experimental dance pieces created specifically for the camera, to live-performance captures from the world's great international stages.

♥ Eat & Drink Near the Castro Theater

If you go to enough film festivals, you will end up at the Castro Theater. The neighborhood is full of drink and dinner spots to extend your date.

- **Canela:** With a wide assortment of Spanish tapas and wines, this warm spot is perfect for a quick bite or a paella to share.

- **Fable:** Featuring one of the best garden patios in the city, this is a great spot before a matinee, but also stays open through dinner.

- **Starbelly:** This California comfort spot is open for weekend brunch, weekday lunch, and daily dinner, making it a good choice whenever your film may show.

- **Anchor Oyster Bar:** Oysters are always a celebration. Also, don't miss the cioppino.

- **Heroic Italian:** Nestled inside the Swirl on Castro wine shop, with a parklet as well as several tables on the sidewalk and limited indoor seating, these sandwiches will keep you full even through a double bill. Note that they close early, so pre-movie only.

- **Lobby Bar:** Craft cocktails and shareable plates make this a great spot to also share those thoughts you did not whisper during the film.

- **Poesia:** Come for happy hour pre-show (every day from 5 to 6:30pm) at this Italian charmer for agnolotti bites or crostini with home made toasted bread, avocado, grilled prawns, and sesame seeds. Their next-door cafe offers in-house baked desserts, pastries, sweets, focaccia sandwiches, and pizzas.

MUSEUMS

One of the best things about museum dates is that there are tons of things to talk about, but it is also okay to be silent as you contemplate the art. Luckily, San Francisco is home to many museums from art to science and more. And many of them offer free admission at least once a month, often on the first Sunday, Tuesday, or Wednesday.

- **San Francisco Museum of Modern Art (SFMOMA):** Features 170,000 square feet of new and renovated galleries, displaying pieces from its collection of 33,000 modern and contemporary artworks, with an entire floor dedicated solely to photography. You can explore the permanent collection or check out the frequent traveling exhibits. The cafe in the fifth floor sculpture garden is a great spot to stop and discuss what you have seen.

- **Institute of Contemporary Art:** This new kid on the block, opened in Dogpatch in late 2022, is a non-collecting contemporary art museum that prioritizes artists over art holdings, individuals over institutions, and equity and expansion of the canon.

DISCOVER & GO

Those with San Francisco library cards can take advantage of Discover & Go, a program that offers free passes for museums, science centers, zoos, theaters, and other cultural destinations. You simply log in with your library card credentials and browse for passes by date or attractions. Make your reservation and print or download your pass shortly before your visit.

♥ de Young Museum

- **de Young:** Another Golden Gate Park destination, the de Young's collection exceeds 27,000 works and is renowned for its American art from the seventeenth through twenty-first centuries, modern and contemporary art, photography, international textiles and costumes, and art from Africa, Oceania, and the Americas. The Free Saturdays initiative makes it possible for Bay Area residents to explore the de Young's permanent collections for free every Saturday if you live in any of the following counties: Alameda, Contra Costa, Marin, Napa, San Francisco, San Mateo, Santa Clara, Solano, or Sonoma.

♥ California Academy of Sciences

- **California Academy of Sciences:** Home to an aquarium, planetarium, natural history museum, and world-class research and educational programs, the Cal Academy is in Golden Gate Park. Don't miss the Thursday night nightlife series, when adults 21+ can enjoy live music, cocktails, and special activities and entertainment in addition to exploring the entire Academy after dark.

- **Legion of Honor:** Built to commemorate soldiers who died in World War I, the Legion of Honor is a beautiful neoclassical building overlooking Lincoln Park and the Golden Gate Bridge. The museum's collection features more than 4,000 years of ancient and European art. Every Saturday the Legion of Honor offers free general admission to all residents of the nine Bay Area counties. This offer applies only to the permanent collection galleries. Reserve your tickets in advance online.

- **Asian Art Museum:** Located in the Civic Center near City Hall, this museum is home to one of the world's most diverse collections of art and objects from across the Asian continent. Spanning 6,000 years of history, you can enjoy beautiful paintings, sculptures, furniture, textiles, and armor originating from Turkey, China, India, Japan, the Philippines, and more.

- **Contemporary Jewish Museum:** Located downtown near the Museum of African Diaspora and the California Historical Society, the Contemporary Jewish Museum presents dynamic exhibitions and educational programs, exploring contemporary perspectives on Jewish culture, history, and ideas.

- **Exploratorium:** This interactive museum inspires creativity in people of all ages. Explore more than 600 hands-on exhibits and enjoy breathtaking views of the city and bay in the spectacular glass-and-steel Bay Observatory. They offer themed Afterdark evenings for 18+ only, every Thursday night from 6:00–10:00pm.

- **Museum of African Diaspora:** Located downtown, MoAD showcases the history, art, and cultural richness that resulted from the dispersal of Africans throughout the African diaspora.

- **Museum of Craft & Design:** Located in Dogpatch, MCD is dedicated to contemporary practices in craft and design. The museum's mission is to explore the active roles craft and design play in everyday life through original and traveling exhibitions, collaborations with museums from around the world, and hands-on opportunities.

TAKE A CLASS

Whether it is exploring block printing or making a meal, often paired with wine, classes are great ways to have fun while learning together.

- **Jenny Lemons:** This colorful boutique and DIY art school is run by San Francisco-based artist Jennie Lennick. The shop hosts craft workshops in person and online, and sells products created by skilled artisans from jewelry to clothing to screen prints. Classes include felting, watercolors, block printing, and macrame.

- **WorkshopSF:** Located at the corner of Haight and Central in the Upper Haight, WorkshopSF offers affordable DIY classes for adults, taught by local teachers, makers, artists, foodies and DIY'ers. Classes include everything from candle making to watercolors to crafting a glass jar succulent garden.

- **Public Glass:** Start with the Play with Fire class to learn how to manipulate glass, add color, and shape it into a beautiful piece of solid glass art. There is also Hot Glass Cold Beer on select Saturday evenings, a long-running event that combines glass demonstrations, live music, craft beer, and food. For $40 you select your own hand-blown glass created by the artists at Public, drink your fill of beer or wine, and then take your glass home when the evening is over.

- **18 Reasons:** This nonprofit community cooking school aims to empower the community with the confidence and creativity needed to buy, cook, and eat good food every day. At their 18th Street Kitchen in San Francisco, chefs from around the world teach classes, and ticket sales help support free pro-gramming for low-income families. Classes include everything from basic knife skills to Malaysian street food and Detroit-style pizza. Classes generally end with a dinner with wine and beer.

- **San Francisco Center for the Book:** Are these classes a little specialized? Yes. But it would be hard to resist a class like Introduction to Lego Letterpress, where you can play around with the design pos-sibilities that unconventional materials like Legos bring to the table, and leave with a stack of prints.

- **Cheese School of San Francisco:** Located in Ghirardelli Square, this one-room schoolhouse now has an entire floor of its own with an iconic view of the San Francisco Bay. Classes range from an exploration of California Cheese to pizza making.

BOOKSTORES

Visiting a neighborhood favorite or attempting a crawl across the city offers limitless excuses to talk about anything and everything—that's the power of reading!

- **Adobe Books & Arts Cooperative:** Adobe Books is known for carrying rare books, showcasing local artists' work on the walls, and hosting numerous events.

- **Alexander Book Company:** Three floors of books in SoMa.

- **Bird & Beckett Books & Records:** The Glen Park gem features frequent live music, particularly jazz, along with literary events.

- **Borderlands Books:** If you are looking for science fiction, mystery, horror, or fantasy,

BOOK CLUB

Whether it is introducing your favorite books to each other or each choosing a selection or two on a bookstore crawl, reading and talking about the same book can be a great way to connect. Bonus points for pairing the discussion with themed food and drink, homemade or takeout!

this store, now relocated to the Haigh, is the place for you.

- **Book Passage:** This Ferry Building offshoot of the well-known Marin store serves locals and visitors and hosts frequent events.

- **Books and Bookshelves:** Looking for both books and the shelves to hold them? Books and Bookshelves is your stop, especially if you are looking for either poetry and/or customizable wood bookshelves.

- **BookShop West Portal:** A locally-owned, independent bookstore located in the heart of the West Portal, a mainly residential neighborhood with a main drag great for strolling.

- **Christopher's Books:** This small store is well-curated, with fiction and mysteries, as well as nonfiction. Plus, it is a great place to browse while waiting for a table at Plow.

- **City Lights Booksellers & Publishers:** Perhaps the most famous bookstore (and publisher) in the city, City Lights draws locals and tourists alike; see page 56 for more.

- **Dog Eared Books:** Located in the Mission, this is a general interest store with a little of everything, but they specialize in off-beat, small press, and local literature.

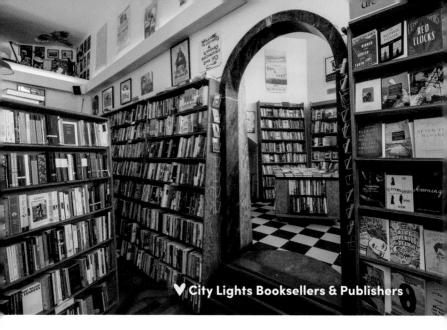

♥ **City Lights Booksellers & Publishers**

- **Fabulosa Books:** A friendly, general interest neighborhood bookstore in the Castro with a large LGBTQ+ section.

- **Green Apple Books:** Founded in 1967, Green Apple has three locations: on Clement Street, Ninth Street near Golden Gate Park and, as Browser Books, on Fillmore in Pacific Heights. It is a store that is nearly perfect for browsing, with frequent author events.

- **Omnivore:** The Bay Area's only culinary bookshop is a must for those who love to cook or read about food. Collections include vintage and antiquarian books, menus, and new releases. They host frequent events, sometimes with food or drink!

- **Books Inc.:** With 10 locations in the San Francisco Bay Area, Books Inc. can trace its history back to 1851, making it the West's oldest independent bookseller. San Francisco locations are at Opera Plaza, Laurel Village, and in the Marina.

- **Booksmith:** This Haight Street store is known for its cozy atmosphere and frequent author readings.

Author Events

- **City Arts and Lectures:** If you are looking for a more formal literary event, with reserved seats in a theater, City Arts is for you. Since 1980, this nonprofit has offered unique programs with leading figures in arts and ideas. Each year there are more than fifty lectures and onstage conversations—and a few surprise performances, film tributes, and concerts—with outstanding writers, critics, scientists, performing artists, and cultural figures from around the world.

- **Writers with Drinks:** Since 2001 this spoken-word variety show, hosted by Charlie Jane Anders at the Makeout Room, has raised money for local causes. The award-winning show includes poetry, stand-up comedy, science fiction, literary fiction, erotica, and memoir.

Too Hard to Categorize, Too Good to Skip

- **Church of John Coltrane:** For over half a century the Saint John Coltrane Global Spiritual Community has been devoted to advocating for social and environmental justice, access to housing, reducing homelessness, and criminal-justice reform. Drop in for Sunday mass at noon for confession, the Coltrane Liturgy, scripture readings, hymns, spirituals, and preaching.

- **Wave Organ:** A wave-activated acoustic sculpture located on a jetty that forms the small Boat Harbor in the Marina. The installation includes 25 organ pipes made of PVC and concrete located at various elevations, allowing for the rise and fall of the tides. Sound is created by the impact of waves against the pipe ends and the subsequent movement of the water in and out of the pipes.

- **Musee Mecanique:** Family-owned since 1933, this is a for-profit interactive museum of twentieth-century penny arcade games and artifacts, located at Fisherman's Wharf. Admission is free, but you'll pay to play.

- **Martuni's:** You can and should belt out show tunes and drink large martinis at this popular piano bar located at the intersection of the Mission, Hayes Valley, the Castro, and the Lower Haight, or as some might say, not that far from Zuni. You'll hear amateurs, but also professionals singing standards and cabaret classics.

♥ Wave Organ

- **Tonga Room:** This sprawling tiki-themed lounge in the Fairmont Hotel features Pacific Rim cuisine and umbrella drinks. It also features thunderstorms every 30 minutes and a pool (not for swimming, though you may be tempted after a few drinks). Is it kitschy? Sure. But after a mai tai or two you'll delight in twirling around the dance floor.

- **American Conservatory Theater:** A.C.T. is a Tony Award–winning nonprofit theater with a mission to engage the spirit of the San Francisco Bay Area, activate stories that resonate, promote a diversity of voices and points of view, and empower theater makers and audiences to celebrate liveness. You can see individual shows, but a season package offers a discount, with preview shows at an additional discount. Why not let a date (at least a good one) last for months?

♥ ACKNOWLEDGMENTS ♥

With thanks to everyone who offered suggestions, read through sections, or simply listened to me during the process, especially Katherine Cleary, Tom Stubbs, Sarah Bedell, the 6 am crew at 17 Reasons, Thea Dwelle, Jeanne Brophy, Lorraine Weston, Eve Batey, Laurie Thomas, Amy Snyder Hale, Alyssa Case, Adrienne DeAngleo, and, of course, Matthew Redmond.

♥ ABOUT THE AUTHOR ♥

A longtime San Francisco resident and fan of alliteration, Amy Cleary has worked in publishing, public relations, and public policy. She has been on many dates, both memorable and quickly forgotten, including an exhausting and exhilarating year of 50 first dates. Her favorite things include sunrises, fried chicken, beach glass, and magnolias.

ABOUT CIDER MILL PRESS BOOK PUBLISHERS

Good ideas ripen with time. From seed to harvest, Cider Mill Press brings fine reading, information, and entertainment together between the covers of its creatively crafted books. Our Cider Mill bears fruit twice a year, publishing a new crop of titles each spring and fall.

"Where Good Books Are Ready for Press"

501 Nelson Place
Nashville, Tennessee 37214

cidermillpress.com